100 Clear Grammar Tests

100 Clear Grammar Tests

Reproducible Grammar Tests
for Beginning to Intermediate
ESL/EFL Classes

Keith S. Folse

Joseph Gabriella

Linda Hadeed

Jeanine Ivone

April Muchmore-Vokoun

Elena Vestri Solomon

Makoto Yoshii

Ann Arbor

THE UNIVERSITY OF MICHIGAN PRESS

To the Teacher

100 Clear Grammar Tests is a set of one hundred reproducible (photocopiable) tests on common grammar points covered in beginning and intermediate ESL grammar books. The tests in this book are intended to accompany *Clear Grammar 1, 2,* and *3.* However, in actuality, the tests are suitable for use with any beginning to intermediate ESL grammar book.

Each grammar point has at least two tests devoted to it. For example, Test 20 and Test 21 cover *wh-* questions, and Test 71 and Test 72 both cover past progressive tense. More difficult grammar points or grammar points that encompass more material may have three or four tests in this book.

Some of the benefits of having multiple tests available for teachers (and learners) include:

1. teachers can find a test that resembles their own teaching style;
2. teachers can find a test that resembles the way the learners expect to be tested;
3. teachers can use one test as a practice test and still have one (or more) for the actual test;
4. learners can see their progress in various ways because the tests use a variety of question types;
5. learners learn in different ways with different styles, so tests with different kinds of questions are a good thing; and
6. learners can have a second (or third) chance with a grammar point if the teacher permits this.

It should be noted that the tests included in this book were written by seven different instructors with seven writing styles, seven teaching styles, and seven testing variations. The reason for this high number of authors was to produce a book of tests that would include a variety not only of types of questions but also of approaches to testing. In many ways, the one hundred tests in this book are different, but in many ways they are similar.

There is no one who knows your teaching situation and your learners better than you do, so it is up to you to choose testing materials that match not only what has been taught, that is, the content, but also the way in which the students were taught, for example, drill, conversation, writing, and the way in which the students are accustomed to being tested. While experimentation and innovation are appropriate to the classroom, learners under the stress of a testing situation may not do well on tests that are outside of what they are expecting.

We have tried to include a wide array of types of questions in the tests. Examples include matching, multiple choice, error location, error correction, completion (filling in the blanks), connecting sentence parts, rearranging word order, grammatical identification (e.g., underline the verbs in these sentences), and manipulation (e.g., change the verbs to past tense). It is important for teachers to make sure that their students are familiar with and as comfortable as possible with the types of questions used in the test. Students may have problems answering a question because they do not know the answer, but they should not have problems answering the question because of the question itself.

For teachers' convenience, there are three ways to access a test for a given grammar point.

1. If you are using the Clear Grammar series, simply look for the book and unit number in the table of contents. For example, if you want to test Unit 4 from Book 2, you would look through the table of contents for that unit number in that particular book. The appropriate tests for Unit 4 in Book 2 are Tests 40 and 41.

2. If you want a test on a specific grammar point but are not using the Clear Grammar series, you should look for the name of the grammar point in the table of contents. For example, if you want a test on articles, you would look down the listing of grammar points until you find the term *articles*. The appropriate tests for articles are Test 35 and Test 36.

3. A third way to access a test on a given grammar point is to use the index at the back of the book. If you want a test on prepositions, you would look through the alphabetized list until you find the term *prepositions,* and then you will find that Test 29 and Test 30 deal with this particular grammar point.

Contents

The following listing gives the test number (which appears at the top of every test), the corresponding volume (book) number and unit number from the Clear Grammar series, and a description of the grammar point.

Contents   ix

Contents   x

TEST 1   Parts of Speech

Clear Grammar 1, Pre-Unit

Name _____   Date _____

Part 1   Underline the nouns in these sentences.

1. Florida, Arizona, and Texas are warm states.

2. Nancy and Jennifer like expensive restaurants.

3. The blue book is under the yellow chair.

4. I usually eat big, red apples for breakfast.

5. The brown dog is happy.

Part 2   Underline the verbs in these sentences.

1. Florida, Arizona, and Texas are warm states.

2. Nancy and Jennifer like expensive restaurants.

3. The blue book is under the yellow chair.

4. I usually eat big, red apples for breakfast.

5. The brown dog is happy.

Part 3   Underline the adjectives in these sentences.

1. Florida, Arizona, and Texas are warm states.

2. Nancy and Jennifer like expensive restaurants.

3. The blue book is under the yellow chair.

4. I usually eat big, red apples for breakfast.

5. The brown dog is happy.

Part 4   The underlined word in each pair of sentences is the same word, but the part of speech (noun, verb, adjective) is different. Write *n* (noun), *v* (verb), or *adj* (adjective) on the lines to tell whether the words are nouns, verbs, or adjectives.

_____adj_____   1. Ann wants to <u>paper</u> her bedroom on Saturday.

_____noun_____   2. Nancy needs to write a <u>paper</u> for school on Monday.

_____adj_____   3. I like to sit in the <u>dark</u>.

_____adj_____   4. Don was afraid to sit in the <u>dark</u> room.

_____verb_____   5. Mohammed asked me to go to the <u>dance</u> on Friday.

_____verb_____   6. Nina likes to swim, but she doesn't like to <u>dance</u>.

TEST 2 Grammatical Terms

Clear Grammar 1, Pre-Unit

Name _____ Date _____

Part 1 Look at the underlined word in each sentence. Write *n* (noun), *v* (verb), or *adj* (adjective) to show what part of speech the word is.

1. _n_ Many <u>ships</u> travel between Miami and Caracas every week.

2. _N_ The number of <u>ships</u> in Miami now is incredible.

3. _V_ That company <u>ships</u> boxes from Miami to Caracas.

4. _V_ Be careful with that knife or you might <u>cut</u> yourself.

5. _N_ If you have a bad <u>cut</u>, you must clean it immediately.

6. _V_ I don't like to <u>cut</u> my grass.

7. _adj_ This <u>test</u> question is too difficult.

8. _N_ This <u>test</u> has many difficult questions.

9. _V_ Teachers <u>test</u> students because it helps students learn.

10. _N_ His job is to put the groceries in plastic <u>bags</u>.

11. _V_ Joseph <u>bags</u> groceries at the supermarket.

12. _N_ A plastic <u>bag</u> is stronger than a paper bag.

Part 2 Write *n, v,* or *adj* above each of the underlined words to show if it is a noun, a verb, or an adjective.

1. The <u>apple</u>[adj] <u>trees</u>[n] in the <u>yard</u>[n] are not very <u>tall</u>[adj].

2. The <u>driver</u>[N] had a <u>cut</u>[N] on his <u>back</u>[N] from the <u>car</u>[adj] <u>accident</u>[N].

3. I didn't <u>back</u>[V] the <u>car</u>[N] into the <u>tree</u>[N], so I didn't cause this <u>accident</u>[N].

4. Please <u>write</u>[V] your <u>complete</u>[adj] <u>name</u>[N] on the <u>back</u>[N] of the <u>test</u>[adj] paper.

5. How many <u>countries</u>[N] in <u>Africa</u>[N] can you <u>name</u>[V]?

TEST 3   Present Tense of *Be*

Clear Grammar 1, Unit 1

Name _____   Date _____

Part 1   Underline the correct words or phrases in this conversation.

Kelly: Hi, Nathan. How ❶ (am, is, are) you?

Nathan: ❷ I ('m, 're, 's) fine. You look tired. ❸ (What's, What're) up?

Kelly: I ❹ (am, is, are) tired. I studied last night for five hours.

Nathan: Why?

Kelly: ❺ (Am, Is, Are) you serious? We have a grammar test today.

Nathan: The grammar test ❻ (am not, isn't, aren't) today.

Kelly: Yes, ❼ (I am, it is, they are).

Nathan: Kelly, the test ❽ (am, is, are) not today.

Kelly: Nathan, ❾ you ('m, 's, 're) wrong. Here comes Dennis. Ask him.

Dennis: Hi, guys. ❿ (How's, How're) it going?

Nathan: ⓫ (Is the grammar test, The grammar test is) today?

Dennis: Why do you ask that question?

Nathan: Kelly says the test ⓬ (am, is, are) today, but I say that ⓭ (am, is, are) not true.

Dennis: Well, Nathan, you ⓮ (am, is, are) wrong. Kelly ⓯ (am, is, are) right. The test
⓰ (am, is, are) at 2:00 today.

Nathan: Oh, no! ⓱ I ('m, 's, 're) in big trouble now!

Clear Grammar 1 (vertical sidebar)

Part 2 Each sentence has three underlined words. One of the words contains an error. Circle the error and write a correction above it.

1. Ontario and Nova Scotia ~~is~~ [are] provinces in Canada.

2. William ~~have~~ [is] hungry now because he didn't eat breakfast or lunch today.

3. January ~~is~~ [has] 31 days, but April and June have 30.

4. *Ann:* Are you ready to eat dinner now?

   Jason: Yes, of course ~~I'm~~ [I am]

5. The name of those mountains are the Himalayas.

6. Bader isn't thirsty, but ~~I'm~~ [I am]

7. I want to buy those curtains because they ~~is~~ [are] very cheap.

8. When the students ~~be~~ [are] late to class, the teacher is extremely angry at them!

9. Canada, the United States, and Mexico ~~in~~ [are] North America.

10. The main reason for all the problems in those three countries are the bad economy.

TEST 4   Present Tense of *Be*

Clear Grammar 1, Unit 1

Name _____   Date _____

Part 1   Fill in the blanks with the correct forms of *be: am, is, are.*

1. Russia _____is_____ a big country.

2. I _____am_____ in bed at 11 P.M. every day.

3. Andrea and I _____are_____ good students.

4. She _____is_____ in the kitchen right now.

5. Mike and Cathy _____are_____ in Washington, D.C., today.

6. They _____are_____ good at math.

7. I _____am_____ very hungry. I want something to eat.

8. The students in the classroom _____are_____ American.

9. The weather _____is._____ very nice today.

10. You _____are_____ from a big city, and I _____ from a small town.

Part 2   Write the two possible short answers for each question.

1. Is John in the bathroom now?

   _____ . OR _____ .

2. Are you and Mary in different classes this semester?

   _____ . OR _____ .

3. Are you thirsty?

   _____ . OR _____ .

4. Is Mrs. Smith the smartest teacher in that school?

   _____ . OR _____ .

5. Is the TOEFL a very difficult test?

   _____ . OR _____ .

Part 3 Write the correct words *(am, is, are)* in the blanks.

1. *A:* "_____ you from China?"

    B: "No, I _____ from China. I _____ from Japan."

    A: "Oh, I see."

2. *A:* "_____ this for here or to go?"

    B: "For here. I want to sit down and eat it now."

3. *A:* "_____ Susan and Lucy college students?"

    B: "No, they _____ college students. They _____ still in high school."

4. *A:* "_____ we going in the right direction?"

    B: "Yes, I think so. I _____ pretty sure that this _____ the right direction."

TEST 5   Present Tense of Regular Verbs

Clear Grammar 1, Unit 2

Name _____   Date _____

Part 1   Read the sentences carefully and then underline the correct form of each verb.

1. Joe (catch, catches) fish every morning from the pier. He (want, wants) to eat fish every night for dinner. Joe and the pelicans (try, tries) to catch the fish first.

2. I (watch, watches) T.V. at 6:30 every evening. I (like, likes) to watch the evening news on Channel 28. The newsperson on that channel (talk, talks) a lot about international news.

3. Susan and James (go, goes) kayaking on the weekends. They (like, likes) to explore the Hillsborough River. The alligators (watch, watches) them.

4. Our tennis team (train, trains) hard to be the best. We (practice, practices) five days a week after school.

5. I (wash, washes) my clothes on Saturday, Mary (do, does) her laundry on Monday, and the twins, Julie and Jennifer, (do, does) theirs on Friday.

6. Steve (play, plays) the guitar very well. He and James (write, writes) the music themselves. The band (perform, performs) in clubs on the weekends.

Part 2   Fill in the blanks with the correct forms of the verbs.

(cook)   1. Do you _____ for yourself every day?

(type)   2. Mark _____ the letters for his boss.

(listen)   3. Marta, Jane, and Paula _____ to their teacher.

(arrive)   4. The plane from New York _____ at 3:00 P.M. on Thursdays.

(like)   5. I _____ to walk in the evenings.

(understand)   6. We _____ Italian when it is spoken slowly.

(deliver)   7. The mail person _____ the mail to my home every day except Sundays.

(use)   8. John _____ a proper car shampoo to wash his car.

(jog)   9. We _____ two miles after lunch every day.

(share)   10. Ahmad and Omar _____ an apartment near the university.

Clear Grammar 1

TEST 6 Present Tense of Regular Verbs

Clear Grammar 1, Unit 2

Name _____   Date _____

Part 1   Fill in the blanks with the correct forms of the verbs.

1. (study) Fred and Chris _____ every day.

2. (write) Nancy _____ an e-mail to her family once a week.

3. (watch) The cat _____ the fish swim in the bowl.

4. (think) Good students _____ of new ways to learn.

5. (know) My father _____ how to speak Italian.

Part 2   Underline the correct negative form of each verb.

1. Lee (don't, doesn't) like to eat sushi.

2. Henri (don't, doesn't) want to travel this month.

3. Oliver and I (don't, doesn't) swim in the ocean.

4. Elias and Ben (don't, doesn't) play well together.

5. Jennifer (don't, doesn't) drink coffee.

Part 3   Multiple Choice. Circle the letter of the correct answer.

1. "_____ your mother like to cook?"

   "Yes, she likes to cook spaghetti."

   (A) Do   (C) Is

   (B) Does   (D) Are

2. "_____ Yoko and Mizuki students?"

   "Yes, they are. They study English."

   (A) Do   (C) Is

   (B) Does   (D) Are

3. "_____ Lee and Ann work at the hotel?"

    "Yes, they do. They work four nights per week."

    (A)   Do   (C)   Is

    (B)   Does   (D)   Are

4. "_____ Michael married to Allison?"

    "Yes, he is. They got married in April."

    (A)   Do   (C)   Is

    (B)   Does   (D)   Are

5. "_____ Jackie like to watch television?"

    "Yes, she does. She watches it every night."

    (A)   Do   (C)   Is

    (B)   Does   (D)   Are

TEST 7   Review

Clear Grammar 1, Units 1 and 2

Name _____ Date _____

Part 1   Underline the correct forms of *be.*

1. Roberto (is, am, are) a student at the university.

2. Suzanne and Brett (is, am, are) married.

3. Barry (is, am, are) an intelligent person.

4. I (is, am, are) a citizen of the United States.

5. Yukiko and Michio (is, am, are) citizens of Japan.

Part 2   Read each sentence. If it is correct, circle C. If it is not correct, circle X and write a correction on the line.

C   X   1.   Nancy no is a student.   _____

C   X   2.   My father isn't Italian.   _____

C   X   3.   This room are not warm.   _____

C   X   4.   The dog not black.   _____

C   X   5.   Susan is not from China.   _____

Part 3   Read the words and then make a question. Use the correct form of *be.*

1. in class / you / (be)   _____

2. in America / your parents / (be)   _____

3. now/ ten o'clock / it / (be)   _____

4. a student / you / (be)   _____

5. in / your seat / I / (be)   _____

Part 4   Read the questions in Part 3. On the lines below, write short answers for those questions.

1. _____

2. _____

3. _____

4. _____

5. _____

Part 5 Write the missing verb forms.

1. I cry, you cry, he _____
2. I watch, you watch, she _____
3. I study, you study, he _____

4. I have, you have, it _____
5. I am, you are, she _____
6. I do, you do, he _____

Part 6 Write three affirmative sentences and three negative sentences. Use a different verb in each sentence. Write true sentences about yourself, your family, your friends, or your classroom.

1. (affirmative) _____
2. (affirmative) _____
3. (affirmative) _____
4. (negative) _____
5. (negative) _____
6. (negative) _____

Part 7 Write the correct words on the lines. Use the correct pronouns and the correct forms of affirmative and negative verbs.

1. (speak) Q: _____ you _____ Russian?

    A: No, _____ Russian. I speak English.

2. (study) Q: _____ your mother _____ biology?

    A: No, _____ biology. _____ botany.

3. (have) Q: _____ your sister _____ a cat?

    A: No, _____ a cat. _____ a dog.

TEST 8   Demonstratives

Clear Grammar 1, Unit 3

Name _____   Date _____

Part 1   Write *this, that, these,* or *those* on the lines. Use the words in parentheses to help you choose the correct answer.

1. (there) ____Those____ dogs are very smart.

2. (here) In ____this____ university, we have seven colleges.

3. (there) Are ____those____ rare books? They look really old.

4. (here) Does she like ____this____ music?

5. (there) ____those____ nine packages are not for you.

6. (here) We don't have ____this____ kind of weather in my country.

7. (there) Everybody knows ____those____ tests are very difficult.

8. (here) ____This____ software is easy to use.

9. (here) ____These____ cars are very expensive.

10. (here) ____This____ cat is male.

Part 2   Write *this, that, these,* or *those* on the lines.

   Situation: Tom and Mike are at a party.

Tom: Hey, Mike. Who is ❶ ____that____ man standing over there?

Mike: Which man?

Tom: ❷ ____That____ man at the counter.

Mike: You mean ❸ ____that____ tall man in the green shirt?

Tom: Yes.

Mike: I don't know. But he came with three other people.

Tom: Really? Which people?

Mike: He came with ❹ ____that____ woman over there by the door. I think she is

        his wife.

Tom: Yes, I see her now.

Mike: And he came with ❺ _those_ two boys over there. I think they are his sons.

Tom: Yes, I think you're right. They are his sons.

Mike: Why do you ask?

Tom: I think his name is Jonathan Yates. If he is Jonathan Yates, then I want to speak to him.

Mike: About what?

Tom: About some business. I want to give him ❻ _this_ envelope. It is especially for him. It has several pages of information about my company.

Mike: OK, good luck!

TEST 9   Demonstratives

Clear Grammar 1, Unit 3

Name _____   Date _____

Part 1   Write *this* or *these* on the lines.

1. _____ spoon

2. _____ spoons

3. _____ steak knife

4. _____ steak knives

5. _____ large suitcase

6. _____ very large suitcases

7. _____ map

8. _____ pictures

Part 2   Write *that* or *those* on the lines.

1. _____ town

2. _____ hills

3. _____ children

4. _____ school

5. _____ sunset

6. _____ wild dogs

7. _____ shopping mall

8. _____ delicious desserts

Part 3   Complete the sentences by underlining the correct words in parentheses.

1. (This, These) car is mine. (That, Those) car belongs to my sister.

2. (This, These) tea is too hot. (That, Those) tea is iced tea.

3. (This, These) sunglasses are broken. (That, Those) are too big.

4. (This, These) disks are yours. (That, Those) disks belong to Aisha.

5. (This, These) computer does not work well, but (that, those) one is much faster.

6. (This, These) classroom is for English. (That, Those) classroom is for science.

7. (This, These) pictures are very modern. (That, Those) pictures are antiques.

8. (This, These) exercises are very easy. (That, Those) exercises in the other book are very hard.

TEST 10 Possessive Adjectives

Clear Grammar 1, Unit 4

Name _____   Date _____

Part 1   Write the correct possessive adjectives on the lines. Use *my, your, his, her, its, our,* or *their.*

1.   I   _____   car

2.   Maria   _____   apartment

3.   they   _____   dog

4.   the dog   _____   bone

5.   you   _____   books

6.   you and I   _____   suitcase

7.   Tom and Jane   _____   garden

8.   she   _____   ball

9.   they   _____   tents

10. he and I   _____   tent

11. our friends   _____   picnic

12. his aunt   _____   horse

13. we   _____   camper

14. your cats   _____   food

15. she and Gina   _____   party

Part 2   Complete the sentences. Use *my, your, her, his, its, our,* or *their.*

1. I am sitting in the den. _____ desk is untidy. I have to clean it soon.

2. Alison and Nicholas are playing in the garden. I can see them now because

    _____ house is next door to mine.

3. My brothers live on the same street as I do. _____ houses are near each

    other, so we can visit each other easily.

4. Peter's Jeep is blue. _____ car has a Wyoming license plate.

5. My sister and I play volleyball for the school team. _____ team is in second

    place.

Clear Grammar 1

6. You have many fishing rods. _____ rods are very expensive.

7. I like to swim every day. _____ pool is heated in the winter.

8. Sarah has two brothers._____ brother Greg goes to college in Kentucky.

    _____ other brother graduated from the University of Texas last month.

9. You are wearing jeans. _____ jeans are torn.

10. The neighbors have two dogs. _____ dogs bark all the time.

TEST 11 Possessive Adjectives

Clear Grammar 1, Unit 4

Name _____   Date _____

Part 1   Read each sentence. If it is correct, write C on the line. If it is not correct, write X on the line and write a correction above the sentence.

_____ 1. He and his brother are handsome.

_____ 2. Jessica her shirt is pretty.

_____ 3. She is a Spanish teacher. His name is Angela.

_____ 4. We house is in Tampa.

_____ 5. Julia and Ursula are German. Their country is in Europe.

Part 2   Underline the correct words.

1. Does Susan like (she, her) roommate?

2. Do you want to come to (I, my) party?

3. (They, Their) house is beautiful.

4. (They, Their) like to decorate the house.

5. (I, My) know your sister.

Part 3   Fill in the blanks with the correct possessive adjectives.

1. She is from Japan. _____ name is Ichiko.

2. I am from the United States. _____ native language is English.

3. Nancy and Henry live in Colorado. _____ favorite sport is skiing.

4. My sister and I love music. _____ favorite musician is Elton John.

5. Eduardo is tired. That's why_____ eyes are closed.

TEST 12   Review

Clear Grammar 1, Units 3 and 4

Name _____   Date _____

Part 1   Write *this, that, these,* or *those* on the lines.

1. (here)   _____ avocados are not ripe. They are still hard.

2. (there)   _____ book is too difficult for me, so I need an easier one to read.

3. (there)   _____ clouds are very dark. I think it will rain soon.

4. (here)   _____ telephone bill is not mine.

5. (here)   _____ theater tickets are very expensive.

6. (there)   _____ purple grapes have seeds in them. I prefer the green ones.

7. (there)   _____ computer has a 19-inch monitor.

8. (here)   My father prefers _____ weekly magazine.

9. (here)   _____ oranges are from Florida. They are really juicy.

10. (there)   The horses like to run in _____ field.

Part 2   Underline the correct words.

1. Did Jane bring (you, your) swimsuit with her?

2. This is (I, my) diary.

3. Where did the letter carrier put (we, our) package?

4. (They, Their) house is on 56th Street.

5. Marta put (she, her) suitcase on top of the car, and it fell off.

6. Tony is working on (he, his) boat at the dock.

Part 3 Read each sentence. If it is correct, write C on the line. If it is not correct, write X on the line and write a correction above the sentence.

_____ 1. This exercise is easy. His understands it.

_____ 2. The cake is delicious. We ate her all.

_____ 3. What is your grade in English?

_____ 4. My house has a large garden and a swimming pool.

_____ 5. You bicycle is very good. It is a mountain bike.

_____ 6. The gardener cuts our grass every week in the summer.

_____ 7. These book are too heavy for me to carry.

_____ 8. That restaurant is very cheap, and the food is delicious.

_____ 9. Those chicken lays eggs every morning.

_____ 10. This earrings are too heavy for my ears.

TEST 13   Past Tense of *Be*

Clear Grammar 1, Unit 5

Name _____   Date _____

Part 1   Read the short passage. Fill in the blanks with the correct form of *be*.

Kareen and I went to a restaurant last night. We both liked the

food very much. Kareen ❶ _____ very happy because the food

❷ _____ not very expensive. A meal at that restaurant is usually

$20 for one person, but last night our dinner ❸ _____ only $25

for the two of us. The meal ❹ _____ excellent. The vegetables

❺ _____ fresh, and the desserts ❻ _____ delicious!

Part 2   Read the short passage. There are five mistakes. Circle the mistakes and write the correct form above the mistakes.

When I was a little girl, my favorite friend is Susan. Susan were very nice to

me. She was very quiet. She don't was loud like some of my other friends. Susan

and I liked to play sports. She were very good at running, and I was very good at

gymnastics. Susan don't were rude to other people. She always spoke nicely to

everybody. Susan was a good person, a good sport, and a good friend.

Part 3   Complete the sentences with the correct negative form of *be*.

1. Karla _____ a good athlete when she was in college.

2. Yangsoon and I _____ happy when we saw our low test scores.

3. Jacqueline and Elias _____ hungry after they ate their candy.

4. Dan _____ comfortable in his new jeans because they were very tight.

5. She _____ married when she graduated. She got married later.

Part 4   Read each statement and then make a *yes/no* question using the word *yesterday*. Write short answers on the lines below the questions.

1. It is hot today.

    Question: _____

    Answer: _____

2. I am late for class today.

    Question: _____

    Answer: _____

3. The teacher is happy today.

    Question: _____

    Answer: _____

4. The news is interesting today.

    Question: _____

    Answer: _____

5. The sky is blue today.

    Question: _____

    Answer: _____

TEST 14   Past Tense of *Be*

Clear Grammar 1, Unit 5

Name _____   Date _____

Part 1   Fill in the blanks with the correct form of *be: am, is, are, was,* or *were.*

1. I _____ there yesterday.

2. Susan and Pat _____ at the coffee shop now.

3. Mr. Jones _____ at the library 20 minutes ago.

4. Mark _____ in the kitchen now.

5. Kate and I _____ at the department store last Sunday.

6. I _____ in my office right now.

7. They _____ at the restaurant an hour ago.

8. She _____ busy at this moment.

Part 2   Complete the sentences with the correct negatives.

1. They didn't do well on the test. They _____ ready for the test.

2. The car _____ a Toyota. It was a Honda.

3. Ms. Smith and Ms. Jones _____ easy teachers last year. The students didn't like them very much.

4. Michael Jordan _____ a football player. He was a basketball player.

5. The class _____ very easy. It was sometimes difficult to understand the teacher.

6. They _____were not_____ in Texas last week. They were in Mexico.

Part 3   Read each statement and then make a question changing the word *today* to *yesterday.*

1. The restaurant is open today.   _____

2. They are busy today.   _____

3. The lions are very sleepy today.   _____

4. The dog is very hungry today.   _____

5. Tim and Mike are very happy today.   _____

TEST 15   Past Tense of Regular and Irregular Verbs

Clear Grammar 1, Unit 6

Name _____   Date _____

Part 1   Write the correct forms of the verbs on the lines.

1. (read)   I _____ the book for two hours yesterday.

2. (do)   Did you _____ the homework?

3. (spend)   She _____ more than three hours on the homework yesterday.

4. (speak)   He _____ to his friends about the accident two days ago.

5. (leave)   I _____ my country for the United States about a year ago.

6. (sell)   I _____ all my books to my friends last year.

7. (choose)   They _____ to study art at a university in Canada.

8. (buy)   She _____ a new car last Sunday. She says that the car runs great.

Part 2   Write the correct verbs in the blanks. Use the correct verb tenses. You may use some verbs more than once.

see	come	go	tell	talk
write	believe	call	bring	study
get	be	have	meet	sleep

1. Last night I ___studied___ for the big vocabulary test for five hours. I also
    ___wrote___ a letter to my parents. My friend Jeremy called me, so we
    ___talked___ on the phone for an hour. He ___told___ me about his life in a
    big city. Before I ___went___ to bed, I ___got___ a glass of milk. Sleeping was
    difficult. In fact, I ___slept___ for only three hours. That's why I'm so tired today.

2. Yesterday I ___went___ to a party. It ___was___ fun. I ___met___ a lot
    of people. People ___came___ and went constantly. I ___saw___ my old
    friend Gloria Jenkins. She and I ___were___ from the same little town in Ohio.
    I couldn't ___believe___ it. This ___brought___ back a lot of memories of my
    home. That night I ___called___ Cathy, my high school sweetheart. I just had
    to hear her voice.

TEST 16 Past Tense of Regular and Irregular Verbs

Clear Grammar 1, Unit 6

Name _____   Date _____

Part 1 Write the past tense forms of the verbs on the lines.

1. I walk   _walked_   9. she talks   _talked_
2. he bakes   _baked_   10. you smile   _smiled_
3. they help   _helped_   11. we listen   _listened_
4. you finish   _finished_   12. I phone   _phoned_
5. it proves   _proved_   13. he cook   _cooked_
6. we need   _needed_   14. I wait   _wait_
7. they enter   _entered_   15. he repeats   _____
8. he shaves   _shaved_   16. she asks   _____

Part 2 Complete the sentences with the past tense of the verbs in parentheses.

1. Leslie (come) ___came___ to my house last night.

2. I (fly) ___flew___ on a 747 on my last trip from Frankfurt to New York.

3. Dana and George (visit) ___visited___ their cousins in Paris twice last year.

4. Millions of years ago, dinosaurs (roam) _____ the face of the earth.

5. The professor (try) ___tried___ to help the students with their papers.

6. We (talk) ___talked___ until 3:00 A.M. last weekend at the Flamingo Club.

7. The little girl (drop) ___dropped___ her ice cream on the floor.

8. The program we (see) ___saw___ last night on television was very interesting.

Part 3 Write the past tense forms of the verbs on the lines.

1. bring _brought._
2. catch _caught._
3. choose _chose._
4. know _knew._
5. eat _ate._
6. lay _laid._
7. think _thought._
8. get _got_
9. fly _flew_
10. have _had_

11. grow _grew._
12. shake _shook_
13. pay _paid._
14. ride _rode_
15. hear _heard._
16. hide _hid_
17. forget _forgot._
18. run _ran_
19. sell _sold_
20. sleep _slept_

Clear Grammar 1, Units 5 and 6

Name _____   Date _____

Part 1 Fill in the spaces below with the correct forms of these verbs. Use the correct verb tenses. You may use some verbs more than once.

take	come	go	drink	spend
be	see	look	have	buy
sit	say	put	wear	give

1. Paul and I ___went___ shopping yesterday. The mall ___was___ very crowded. It ___took___ a long time to find a parking spot. People ___were___ everywhere. We ___spent___ four hours in the mall and ___were___ tired, so we ___drank___ a cup of coffee at a nice coffee shop. We ___bought___ many gifts for our friends and family.

2. I ___had___ a dream last night. In the dream a man ___came___ to my house. He ___wore___ a red outfit. He ___is___ a big man. He ___sat___ on a sofa and relaxed. He ___said___ , "Do you have any wishes?" I ___said___ , "Yes, I want to be able to speak English." He ___looked___ me in the eyes and ___took___ his hand inside a huge bag. He ___took___ out a book and ___put___ it to me. I ___was___ so excited when I ___saw___ the title of the book. It ___was___ *Clear Grammar.*

Part 2 Answer these questions using short negative answers.

1. Did you study last night?

   No, _____.

2. Were they tired yesterday?

   No, _____.

3. Was he a movie star?

   No, _____ .

4. Did Suzy and Mike have a good time at the party?

   No, _____ .

5. Did you understand the speaker's English?

   No, _____ .

TEST 18 Review

Clear Grammar 1, Units 1–6

Name _____   Date _____

Part 1 Each sentence contains an error. Circle the incorrect part and write the correction above it.

1. France and England ~~two~~ *are.* countries in Europe.

2. I ~~no am~~ *(m not)* hungry because I ate dinner at 5:00.

3. My favorite color for pants ~~are~~ *is.* black.

4. *Are* ~~Do~~ you hungry?

5. You ~~in~~ *are* America?

Part 2 Read each sentence. If it is correct, write C on the line. If it is not correct, write X on the line and write a correction above the sentence.

_____ 1. Does your parents speak English?

_____ 2. Is your brother like to dance?

_____ 3. Louis doesn't like to eat asparagus.

_____ 4. Do you want to travel? No, I am not.

_____ 5. My mother doesn't plays the piano.

Part 3 Write *this, that, these,* or *those* on the lines. Use the words in parentheses to help you choose the correct answer.

1. (here)   Do you like _____ book?

2. (there)   _____ students are from Italy.

3. (here)   _____ cats are very beautiful.

4. (there)   _____ car is very expensive.

5. (here)   _____ class is very interesting.

Part 4 Underline the correct words.

1. (My, I) test score is 90.

2. (Our, We) father is out of town.

3. (His, He) loves to play tennis.

4. (Her, She) cat weighs 10 pounds.

5. (Their, They) study hard to learn English quickly.

Part 5 Read each sentence. If it is correct, write C on the line. If it is not correct, write X on the line and write a correction above the sentence.

_____ 1. Today it is hot, but yesterday it is not very hot.

_____ 2. After I finished my homework yesterday, I was very tired.

_____ 3. I no was happy before I learned how to use the computer.

_____ 4. You were sad yesterday?

_____ 5. Was your sister good at math when she was young?

Part 6 Write the past tense forms of the verbs below.

1. study _____
2. watch _____
3. play _____
4. stop _____
5. dance _____

6. need _____
7. try _____
8. hop _____
9. hope _____
10. wish _____

Part 7 Read the words and then write past tense questions. Write negative answers on the lines below the questions.

1. you / like to dance / when you were in junior high school

   Question: _____

   Answer: _____

2. your mother / cook for you / when you were young

   Question: _____

   Answer: _____

3. your parents / call you / last night

   Question: _____

   Answer: _____

4. your mother and father / speak English at home / when you were young

   Question: _____

   Answer: _____

5. your grandparents / visit America / before you were born

   Question: _____

   Answer: _____

TEST 19   Review

Clear Grammar 1, Units 1–6

Name _____   Date _____

Part 1   If the underlined verb is wrong, write the correct verb form above it. If it is correct, write C above it.

Kevin has his grammar test in his hand. He <u>is not</u> happy. He <u>receive</u> a very bad grade on this test. In fact, he <u>fails</u> the test. He <u>write</u> the wrong answer for half of the questions, so his score on this test was only 50 percent. If you <u>want</u> to pass a grammar test at this school, you have to get at least 70 percent correct. Kevin <u>is</u> usually a good student. He usually studies very hard, but Kevin <u>didn't study</u> for this test. The night before the test, Kevin <u>no feel</u> well. He <u>have</u> a bad headache. He <u>took</u> some aspirin, but the aspirin <u>no help</u>. Now Kevin <u>is</u> worried because his grade on the test was so bad. He <u>want</u> to take the test again if the teacher will let him do this.

Part 2   Underline the correct words in this conversation.

Doctor: Hi, Dan. How are you today?

Dan: Not so good. I hurt (this, my, the) back.

Doctor: Really? How did you do (that, these)?

Dan: I picked up a heavy box, and I felt something strange in (the, my, this) back.

Doctor: Is it the first time that you've had (these, this) problem?

Dan: No, sometimes I have problems with (my, his, those) shoulders.

Doctor: Tell me again—what did you pick up?

Dan: It was a box. A woman at work had a heavy box and needed some help. I picked up (my, her, those) box and put it in (my, her, those) car.

Doctor: How much did (this, that) box weigh?

Dan: About 40 pounds.

Doctor: (That, Those) is a lot to pick up.

Dan: At the time, the pain wasn't too strong, but now it really hurts.

Doctor: Here are some pills that should help with the pain. Take two of (this, these) pills before you go to bed and get a lot of rest. If you don't feel better in three or four days, call me again.

Dan: OK. Thanks, doctor.

Doctor: Don't forget. If you don't feel better, call (that, those, my) office and make another appointment. It's important to take care of (those, your, these) problem as quickly as possible.

Clear Grammar 1, Unit 7

Name _____   Date _____

Part 1 Underline the correct word in these conversations.

1. *A:* (Where, What, Why) do you usually eat for lunch?

    B: Not much. I often skip lunch.

2. *A:* Excuse me. I'm looking for Jim Gulikson.

    B: Gee, I don't know. Hey, Sarah. (Where, When, Whom) is Jim?

    C: Sorry, but I don't know.

3. *A:* I like these watches.

    B: Yes, but (when, why, which) watch do you like the best?

4. *A:* (Why, Where, Which) do you want to go to the bank now?

    B: Because I don't have enough money.

5. *A:* (Which, When, What) is your new address?

    B: It's 1493 Nelwood Road.

Part 2 Circle the error in each sentence. Write a correction on the line.

1. What means huge?   _____

2. Where you worked last year?   _____

3. Where did you born?   _____

4. When the grammar exam is?   _____

5. Why Samantha did that?   _____

Part 3   Write *wh-* questions for these answers about Karen Morales.

1.   *A:* _____

     B: Her new phone number is 555-2291.

2.   *A:* _____

     B: She's a doctor.

3.   *A:* _____

     B: She works at Memorial General Hospital.

4.   *A:* _____

     B: She was born on March 10, 1970.

5.   *A:* _____

     B: Dr. Pearson was her favorite professor in medical school.

TEST 21   *Wh-* Questions

Clear Grammar 1, Unit 7

Name _____   Date _____

Part 1   Fill in each blank with the correct question word: *who, what, where, when, which,* or *why.*

1. Q: _____Where_____ do you live?

   A: I live in Michigan.

2. Q: _____when_____ is the winter holiday?

   A: It is in December.

3. Q: _____who_____ is your teacher?

   A: My teacher is Ms. Hudson.

4. Q: _____why_____ do you want to learn English?

   A: I want to learn English because it will help me professionally.

5. Q: _____which_____ is your favorite color?

   A: My favorite color is blue.

Part 2   Make questions by substituting *who, what, why, when,* and *where* for the underlined words.

1. Valerie's major is <u>French</u>.   _____

2. The dog is <u>in the garden</u>.   _____

3. I go to sleep <u>at 11:00</u>.   _____

4. <u>Mr. Garlitz</u> is my favorite teacher.   _____

5. Nina eats chocolate <u>because it is delicious</u>. _____

Part 3 Multiple Choice. Circle the letter of the correct answer.

1. "_____ is your phone number?"

   "My phone number is 555-4127."

   (A) Which   (C) Where

   (B) What   (D) When

2. "When _____?"

   "My birthday is September 30th."

   (A) was your birthday   (C) is your birthday

   (B) is his birthday   (D) your birthday is

3. "_____ to the doctor?"

   "I went to the doctor because I felt sick."

   (A) Why did you go   (C) When did you go

   (B) Where did you go   (D) With whom did you go

4. "_____ mathematics?"

   "I study mathematics at Davis Community College."

   (A) Where you study   (C) When do you study

   (B) Why do you study   (D) Where do you study

5. "_____ book is your favorite?"

   "I like *Charlotte's Web.*"

   (A) When   (C) Why

   (B) Which   (D) Who

Name _____   Date _____

Part 1   Write complete sentences using the words below. Pay attention to word order.

1. dinner / We eat / at 6:00 P.M. / in the kitchen

   we eat dinner in the kitchen at 6:00 p.m

2. study / I / in Tampa / at the University of South Florida

   I study at the u... in Tampa

3. lives / My sister / on Fowler Ave. / in an apartment

   My sister lives in an apartment on fowler.

4. is / at 11:00 / My appointment / in the morning

   My appointment is in the morning at 11:00

5. in the refrigerator / The apples were / yesterday

   T F

Part 2   Put these sentence parts in correct order. Write the new sentences on the lines.

1. in a / house / lived / in 1970 / we / on Fletcher Ave. / small

   We lived in a small house on Fletcher A in 1970

2. bought / a / my brother / boat / year / last / big

   My brother baught a big boat last year

3. in her new kitchen / baked / cake / Nora / delicious / a / night / last

   Nora baked in her new kitchen last night

4. has / garden / my mother / a / large

   My mother has a large garden

5. my / has / sister / house / a / blue

   My sister has a blue house

Part 3 Read each sentence. If it is correct, write C on the line. If it is not correct, write X on the line and write a correction above.

X̶ 1. I live in a house large.

X̶ 2. These are cookies delicious.

✓ 3. Clara has beautiful roses in her garden.

            here
X̶ 4. Please come at noon here.

✓ 5. My shoes are under my bed in my room.

X̶ 6. I study English at a university large.

X̶ 7. I hungry.

✓ 8. Jessica loves chocolate cookies.

✓ 9. Mike drives a yellow cab.

_____ 10. Are expensive these shoes.

TEST 23   Word Order

Clear Grammar 1, Unit 8

Name _____   Date _____

Part 1   Write complete sentences using the words below. Pay attention to word order.

1.   at 5 P.M. / she has / at the university / class

  _She has class a 5PM at _____

2.   here / after class / he has / lunch

  _He has lunch here after class_____

3.   in the room / is / the book / on the table

  _The book is on the table in _____

4.   in a house / on 50th Street / they live

  _They live in a house on _____

5.   I drink / in the morning / coffee / in my office

  _I drink coffee in the morning in my _____

6.   likes to sit / Ms. Robinson / in first class / on a 747

  _Ms. Robinson likes to sit on a 747 in first class_____

7.   they use / every day / software / in the computer lab

  _They use software in the computer lab every day_____

8.   she / small / in / lives / a / house

  _She lives in a small house_____

9.   dinner / we often eat / in the Indian restaurant / at the same table / on Main Street

  _We often eat dinner at the same table in the Indian restaurant on Main S___

10. every day / from 4 to 5 / he practices / typing

  _He practices typing from 4 to 5 every day_____

Part 2   Read this short passage. There are three phrases that are unusual English. In these three phrases, the word order is somewhat strange. Underline the phrases and write the corrections above them.

Stephanie is my best friend. On Siena Street she lives. She has a large house
blue. This house is new. She likes in the morning to read a newspaper. She enjoys
cooking. She always cooks scrambled eggs for breakfast. She eats breakfast after
she reads the newspaper.

TEST 24 Review

Clear Grammar 1, Units 7 and 8

Name _____   Date _____

Part 1 Fill in each blank with the correct question word: *who, what, when, where, which,* or *why*.

1. Q: "_____What_ Who_ are your favorite actors?"

    A: "Sylvester Stallone and Dustin Hoffman are."

2. Q: "_____where_____ do you live?"

    A: "I live in Los Angeles on Loyola Street."

3. Q: "_____why_____ do you eat slowly?"

    A: "I eat slowly because I want to lose weight."

4. Q: "_____what_____ did you eat for dinner last night?"

    A: "I ate pizza and a salad."

5. Q: "_____when_____ do you want to go to the mall?"

    A: "I want to go at 1:00."

Part 2 Read each sentence. If it is correct, write C on the line. If it is not correct, write X on the line and write a correction above the sentence.

_____   1. Q: "Where does your mother live?"

                A: "She lives in Paris."

_____   2. Q: "When do you go to sleep at night?"

                A: "In my room."

_____   3. Q: "What means *fib?*"

                A: "It means a small lie that is not important."

_____ 4. *Q:* "Why do you listen to rock music?"

        A: "I listen to it because I like the rhythm."

_____ 5. *Q:* "What do Suzanne has in the box?"

        A: "She has some books and some pencils."

Part 3   Put these sentence parts in correct order. Write the new sentences on the lines.

1. apartment / small / live / I / in / a

_____

2. was born / I / July 18th / at / 10:00 A.M. / on

_____

3. in the library / Maria studies / psychology / every night

_____

4. to class / every day / the students / go

_____

5. bought / beautiful / Fred / a / dog

_____

Part 4   Read each sentence. If it is correct, write C on the line. If it is not correct, write X on the line and write a correction above the sentence.

_____ 1. Diana bought three small rings.

_____ 2. These are beautifuls glasses.

_____ 3. The blue chair is very comfortable.

_____ 4. Margo has two dogs small.

_____ 5. In this school David teaches every day.

TEST 25   Present Progressive Tense

Clear Grammar 1, Unit 9

Name _____   Date _____

Part 1   Write each expression in the present progressive tense. Put an X by the verbs that you cannot use in present progressive.

1. they stand   _____
2. you say   _____
3. I remember   _____X_____
4. he listens   _____
5. they like   _____X_____

6. she prefers   _____X_____
7. I repeat   _____
8. we take   _____
9. you possess   _____X_____
10. she hears   _____X_____

Part 2   Write the correct form of the verb in each sentence.

(eat)
1. He can't repair your car now. He _____ lunch.
2. He _____ four meals a day.

(write)
3. Before I go to bed, I usually _____ in my diary.
4. I _____ a letter to my parents now.

(believe)
5. I didn't _____ the news two days ago.
6. I _____ the news now.

(use)
7. Joan _____ the computer every day.
8. Joan's brother _____ the computer now.

(need)
9. Students don't usually _____ the teacher's help in the lab.
10. The students _____ the teacher's help in the lab now.

TEST 26   Present Progressive Tense

Clear Grammar 1, Unit 9

Name _____   Date _____

Part 1   Write the correct form of the verb in each sentence.

(study)   1.   Brett is in his room now. He _____ science.

2.   Brett _____ every day.

(drink)   3.   Maxwell _____ eight glasses of water every day.

4.   Maxwell can't talk now. He _____ water.

(eat)   5.   Nina _____ sushi once a week.

6.   Nina can't come with us. She _____ sushi now.

(listen)   7.   Mike _____ to the news now. He wants to hear the weather.

8.   Mike _____ to the news every day.

(play)   9.   Alison _____ with her children now.

10.   Alison _____ with her children every day after work.

Part 2   Write a question using the words below. Then write a short answer. If it is possible, use the present progressive tense. If it is not possible to use the present progressive tense, use the simple present tense.

1.   Yoko and Ichiko—speak English—with each other   (Yes)

Q: _Are Yoko and Ichiko speaking with each other?_____

A: _Yes, they are_____

2.   it—rain—now   (No)

Q: _Is it raining now?_____

A: _No, it isn't_____

3.   you—love—your mother   (Yes)

Q: _Does your mother love you?_____

A: _Yes, she does_____

4. you—need—food and water   (Yes)

Q: _Do you need food and water?_

A: _Yes, I do_

5. Steven—watch—television   (No)

Q: _Is Steven watching TV_

A: _No, he isn't_

Part 3 Read each sentence. If it is correct, write C on the line. If it is not correct, write X on the line and write a correction above the sentence.

_____ 1. Elaine is teaching in Cooper Hall right now.

_____ 2. The cats no are eating their food right now.

_____ 3. I'm needing a new car.

_____ 4. Does Sheila going to the store now?

_____ 5. The students like to dance.

Part 4 Write each verb in the present progressive tense. Be careful with your spelling. Put an X by the verbs that you cannot usually use in the present progressive tense.

1. open   _____   6.   watch   _____

2. sit   _____   7.   love   _____

3. want   _____   8.   help   _____

4. eat   _____   9.   remember _____

5. dance   _____   10. like   _____

TEST 27   Count vs. Noncount

Clear Grammar 1, Unit 10

Name _____   Date _____

Part 1   Underline the correct forms in these conversations.

1. *A:* I am really thirsty. Do you have anything to drink?

    B: Yeah. I have (some, any, a few) iced tea. Let me make you a glass.

2. *A:* I want to make (an, some) apple pie for dessert.

    B: There are two apples in the refrigerator.

    A: Only two? We need (a few, a little) more apples to make a really good pie.

3. *A:* We are going out for dinner tonight. Do you want to come with us?

    B: No, thanks. Maybe next time. I don't have (much, many) money right now.

4. *A:* Excuse me. Where can I find salt in this store?

    B: I'm sorry. I don't think we have (some, any) salt. Let me check for you.

    A: Thank you.

5. *A:* Wow! Look at that family over there!

    B: They sure have (much, a lot of) children!

Part 2   Multiple Choice. Circle the letter of the correct answer.

1. *Elena:*   Did you have any homework last night?

    Keith: Yes, the teacher gave us _____ homework.

    (A)   many   (C)   any

    (B)   much   (D)   a lot of

2. *Makoto:*   I need a cup of _____ to make this cake. Can you get it for me?

    Sally: Yes. Here you go.

    (A)   sugar   (C)   sand

    (B)   bread   (D)   tea

3. Rita is a vegetarian. She won't eat _____ meat at all.

    (A)   many   (C)   any

    (B)   much   (D)   a lot of

4. *Linda:* I want to hang this poster on my wall. Where are the tacks?

    Irene: I think there are _____ in the kitchen drawer.

    (A) a little   (C) a few

    (B) one   (D) a lot of

5. *Melinda:* Where did you buy that shirt?

    Karen: At the mall. It has everything. There are a lot of great _____ there.

    (A) thing   (C) shirt

    (B) money   (D) stores

Part 3 Circle the error in each sentence. Write a correction on the line.

1. They ate much fried chicken for dinner.   _____

2. There is many people at the party.   _____

3. Bob has very difficult writing class.   _____

4. There are a books about English in the library. _____

5. The teacher doesn't need some help.   _____

TEST 28   Count vs. Noncount

Clear Grammar 1, Unit 10

Name _____   Date _____

Part 1   Write *a, an,* or *some* on the lines.

1. They didn't have _____ *some* _____ problem with the decision.

2. I put _____ *some* _____ cream in my coffee.

3. English is _____ *an* _____ international language.

4. Do you have _____ *some* _____ Japanese money with you?

5. We have _____ *an* _____ exam tomorrow.

6. There are _____ *some* _____ apples on the table.

7. I can finish this in _____ *a* _____ minute.

Part 2   Write *many* or *much* on the lines.

1. He is a man of _____ words.

2. Children usually don't drink _____ coffee.

3. When you travel, don't carry _____ cash.

4. This homework will not take _____ time.

5. I've never seen so _____ people.

6. They need to buy _____ textbooks.

7. Do you usually need _____ help from the teacher?

Part 3   Write *a few* or *a little* on the lines.

1. I'm going to California with _____ friends.

2. She has _____ dollars in her pocket.

3. There is _____ time left to study before the exam.

4. They had _____ trouble with food when they first came to America.

5. He likes to put _____ lemon in his iced tea.

6. The army needs _____ good men and women.

7. You only have _____ days to finish your holiday shopping.

TEST 29 Prepositions

Clear Grammar 1, Unit 11

Name _____   Date _____

Part 1 Read the story below. Fill in the blanks with the correct word: *in, at,* or *on.*

My best friend, Marilyn, and I have a lot in common. We were both born ❶ _____on_____ June 22nd. However, Marilyn was born ❷ _____in_____ 1967, and I was born ❸ _____in_____ 1968. We lived ❹ _____on_____ Green Street when we were children but never ❺ _____on_____ the same time. We went to the same high school ❻ _____in_____ Kearney, Nebraska. However, Marilyn left after one year. We studied ❼ _____at_____ the University of Nebraska, but we didn't take the same classes. We got married ❽ _____ the same place ❾ _____ different days. It is very strange that we didn't meet each other until we started working ❿ _____ the same hospital. However, I am glad that we finally met each other and became good friends!

Part 2 Answer the questions below. Write in complete sentences. Use *in, at, on.*

1. When were you born?

    _____

2. Where do you live? (city)

    _____

3. What time do you get up every day?

    _____

4. Where do you study English?

    _____

5. Where is your school located? (street name)

    _____

Part 3 Circle the error in each sentence. Write a correction on the line.

1. I live on 1307 Clifford Avenue.   _____

2. Call me at the morning.   _____

3. Bob lives at Paris.   _____

4. I don't like to go out in the night.   _____

5. We need to meet them in 5:00.   _____

TEST 30   Prepositions

Clear Grammar 1, Unit 11

Name _____   Date _____

Part 1   Write the correct prepositions on the lines.

1. _____ 6 P.M.   6. _____ December 16

2. _____ Taco Bell   7. _____ Friday

3. _____ 1998   8. _____ Florida

4. _____ January   9. _____ noon

5. _____ 3245 Hastings Street   10. _____ Canada

Part 2   Write *at, on,* or *in* on the lines.

1. They usually have a meeting _____ Monday.

2. Can you reach the book _____ the top shelf?

3. Thanksgiving Day is _____ the fourth Thursday _____ November.

4. I've just put some paper _____ the printer.

5. Even _____ December, it's not very cold in Florida.

6. I need to get some money _____ the bank.

7. Let's have lunch together _____ noon tomorrow.

8. My apartment is _____ 56th Street.

9. My favorite TV show starts _____ 8 P.M. _____ Monday.

10. Don't forget your mother's birthday. It's _____ March 16th.

Clear Grammar 1 (sidebar)

Clear Grammar 1, Units 9–11

Name _____   Date _____

Part 1   Write the correct form of the verb in each sentence.

(study)   1.   I usually _____ English for at least two hours a day.

            2.   I can't watch the movie because I _study_ for a test right now.

(have)   3.   The school _____ a new computer lab now.

            4.   The university _____ ten colleges.

(explain)   5.   Mr. Smith is a good teacher. He always _____ the content very well.

            6.   He _____ the grammar right now, but I just don't get it.

(want)   7.   We _____ to study English and communicate in that language.

            8.   They _____ to get a score of 500 on TOEFL now.

Part 2   Underline the correct quantity words.

1.   I don't have (much, a few) milk in the refrigerator.

2.   You are not supposed to eat (many, a lot of) oily food.

3.   Living expenses in that country are cheap. You only need (a little, a few) money every day.

4.   I had (a few, a little) trouble reading the map.

5.   Do you have (much, many) English books at home?

6.   I don't buy (many, a lot of) meat at the store.

7.   I'm worried. There's only (a little, a few) time until the final exam.

8.   He didn't know (many, much) French words, so he couldn't communicate with French people when he went to France last year.

Part 3 Write *at, on,* or *in* on the lines.

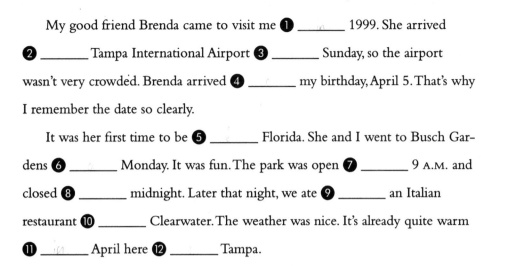

My good friend Brenda came to visit me ❶ _____ 1999. She arrived ❷ _____ Tampa International Airport ❸ _____ Sunday, so the airport wasn't very crowded. Brenda arrived ❹ _____ my birthday, April 5. That's why I remember the date so clearly.

It was her first time to be ❺ _____ Florida. She and I went to Busch Gardens ❻ _____ Monday. It was fun. The park was open ❼ _____ 9 A.M. and closed ❽ _____ midnight. Later that night, we ate ❾ _____ an Italian restaurant ❿ _____ Clearwater. The weather was nice. It's already quite warm ⓫ _____ April here ⓬ _____ Tampa.

TEST 32   Review of Book 1

Clear Grammar 1, Units 1–12

Name _____   Date _____

Part 1   Multiple Choice. Circle the letter of the correct answer.

1. _____ Jan like to work here?

   (A) Is   (C) Do

   (B) Are   (D) Does

2. _____ you and your sister happy in this country?

   (A) Is   (C) Do

   (B) Are   (D) Does

3. _____ your father in the United States?

   (A) Is   (C) Do

   (B) Are   (D) Does

4. _____ Lee and Ann like to dance?

   (A) Is   (C) Do

   (B) Are   (D) Does

5. _____ Amy and Lou in class now?

   (A) Is   (C) Do

   (B) Are   (D) Does

Part 2   Write *this, that, these,* or *those* on the lines. Use the words in parentheses to help you choose the correct answer.

(here)   1.   I need to read _____ book.

(there)   2.   _____ dog is similar to my dog.

(here)   3.   _____ cats are very cute!

(there)   4.   I want to buy _____ shoes.

(here)   5.   Do you like _____ music?

Part 3 Underline the correct words.

1. Do you like (you, your) teacher?

2. (They, Their) child is beautiful.

3. (I, My) know how to speak English.

4. (We, Our) mother is in Italy.

5. (He, His) loves to play football.

Part 4 Read each sentence. If it is correct, write C on the line. If it is not correct, write X on the line and write a correction above the sentence.

_____ 1. The food at the restaurant no was very good.

_____ 2. I was walk to school with my sister yesterday.

_____ 3. Does Emily study French?

_____ 4. I cryed when I watched the movie.

_____ 5. I don't was in class yesterday.

Part 5 Write *wh-* questions using the words below. Pay attention to word order.

1. sister / little / is / where / your _Where is your little sister?_
2. English / why / studying / you / are _Why are y studying E?_
3. actor / who / is / favorite / your _Who's your favorite actor?_
4. birthday / is / your / when _When is your birthday?_
5. *startle* / mean / does / what _What does startle mean?_

Part 6 Write a question using the words below. Then write a short answer. If it is possible to do so, use the present progressive tense. If it is not possible to use the present progressive tense, use the simple present tense.

1. Juan and Manuel—speak Spanish—now (Yes)

    Q: _Are Juan and Manuel speaking spanish now?_
    A: _Yes, they are_

2. your mother—like—asparagus (No)

    Q: _Does your mother like asparagus?_
    A: _No, she doesn't_

3. Ann—want—a gift (Yes)

   Q: _Does Ann want to a gift?_

   A: _Yes, she does_

4. it—snow—now (No)

   Q: _Is it snowing now?_

   A: _No, it isn't_

5. Ryan—play—football (Yes)

   Q: _Does Ryan playing football_

   A: _Yes, he does_

Part 7 Read each sentence. If the underlined part is correct, write C on the line. If it is not correct, write X on the line and write a correction above the sentence.

_____ 1. The teacher gave us <u>a few homeworks</u>.

_____ 2. I don't have <u>much books</u>.

_____ 3. She has <u>a few pencils</u>. Maybe she will give us one.

_____ 4. I drink <u>a lot of coffee</u> because I love it.

_____ 5. Brett has <u>beautiful new car</u>.

Part 8 Fill in the blanks with the correct prepositions.

1. I was born _____ July.

2. Our class begins _____ 9:00 _____ the morning.

3. School begins _____ the fall.

4. The hotel is located _____ Michigan Ave. _____ Chicago.

5. Our graduation dinner was _____ Bennigan's _____ State Street.

TEST 33   Review of Book 1

Clear Grammar 1, Units 1–12

Name _____   Date _____

Error Correction   Each sentence has one grammatical (error) that you have studied.
Circle the error and write a correction above the error.

1. Mrs. Nelson has a beautiful flowers garden.

2. My favorite color *isn't* doesn't green.

3. Does Rita have *her* she suitcase with her?

4. When I was in elementary school, everyone *wore* weared a uniform every day.

5. Do your car have a CD player in it?

6. *Is* Does Monica from Turkey?

7. I don't like these colors for men's shirts.

8. *Does* Is Zina speak English very well?

9. The names of the two best students in my class *are* is Mariana and Mohamad.

10. He put those books in the box, and I took them to the library.

11. There are *some* any sandwiches on the table for you.

12. This computer and those stereo *that* belong to Lina.

13. Abraham Lincoln *was* were the president of the United States during the Civil War.

14. Both Wes and Charlene prefer to live near *their* they're parents.

15. Do you have *any* much brothers and sisters?

16. If you want help with your homework, you can call me at *my* work number.

17. All the students in my math class fail the final exam yesterday.

18. The students are not happy when they saw the test yesterday. *weren't*

19. What did you go on your last vacation? *where*

20. The most dangerous animal in the tropical areas of those countries a small spider.

21. I didn't understood the lesson in grammar class yesterday.

22. I am not knowing the answer to that question. *don't know*

23. The driving test in that state is not an examination difficult.

24. Where did you go on January? *in*

25. Carol prefers to study in the night because her roommate is not usually there. *at night*

26. Most young people like very much that kind of music. *very much*

27. What book do you reading in your English class this week? *Are*

28. When we went to France, we had wonderful time there. *a*

29. We don't had a good time at the beach last Sunday because the weather was bad. *didn't have*

30. Did you able to find your keys last night? *were*

31. Where you learned English? *Do*

32. The grammar class no is very interesting. *is not*

33. When flight number 882 arrived? *Did*

34. His dessert favorite is chocolate cake with vanilla ice cream on top.

35. I can't go to the store with you because I help my father now. *am helping*

36. Luke and Ursula prefer to shop there in Monday. *on*

TEST 34   Review of Book 1

Clear Grammar 1, Units 1–12

Name _____   Date _____

Multiple Choice   Circle the letter of the correct answer.

1. "Tim _____ in a house."

   "No, that isn't true. Tim lives in an apartment."

   (A)   lived   (C)   live

   (B)   lives   (D)   was live

2. "That sentence is very short."

   "Yes, you're right. This sentence _____ have many words."

   (A)   am not   (C)   don't

   (B)   doesn't   (D)   isn't

3. "Was the food good at the restaurant?"

   "_____ . I enjoyed it very much."

   (A)   No, it wasn't.   (C)   No, I wasn't.

   (B)   Yes, it was.   (D)   Yes, I was.

4. "Is Kate a good student?"

   "No, she isn't. She _____ ."

   (A)   don't have a book   (C)   don't do her homework

   (B)   doesn't try hard   (D)   doesn't studies much

5. "_____ write letters to?"

   "Susan."

   (A)   Who you   (C)   Who do you

   (B)   Whom you   (D)   Whom you do

6. "_____ book did you like the best?"

   (A)   Which   (C)   Why

   (B)   Whom   (D)   When

7. "Are you studying English at school?"

"No, _____ ."

(A) you are   (C) you aren't

(B) we are   (D) we aren't

8. "Grammar class is very difficult. I _____ that class very well."

(A) am not understanding   (C) do not understand

(B) am not understand   (D) don't understanding

9. "It wasn't cold today, and I wanted some fresh air, so I _____ the window."

(A) was open   (C) open

(B) was opened   (D) opened

10. "I really want to read a good book in English."

"I have some books here on this shelf. Do you want to borrow one of

_____ books?"

(A) these   (C) those

(B) this   (D) that

11. "What are you going to get from the store?"

"I'm going to buy a loaf of _____ ."

(A) meat   (C) sugar

(B) bread   (D) cheese

12. "Does Walter have a car?"

"Yes, he does. _____ is a gray Toyota Celica."

(A) He car new   (C) His new car

(B) He new car   (D) His car new

13. "Where does Mr. Brown live?"

"He lives on _____ ."

(A) 1234 Sunset Avenue   (C) Chicago

(B) Sunset Avenue   (D) Chicago, Illinois

14. "Oh, there's Betsy. I _____ her now."

(A) see   (C) am not see

(B) am seeing   (D) don't seeing

15. "What did you do during the holiday?"

"Not much. We _____ very busy."

(A) didn't   (C) don't

(B) wasn't   (D) weren't

16. "Let's work on the project at _____ ."

"All right. That sounds good to me."

(A) June 12   (C) the afternoon

(B) Sunday   (D) 4:00

17. "We have our _____ on Monday."

(A) there English classes   (C) English classes there

(B) there classes English   (D) classes English there

18. "I need a pen to fill out this form."

"Oh, I think I have _____ pen in my bag. Let me check."

(A) a   (C) any

(B) an   (D) some

19. "Was the test very long?"

"Yes, it was. At the end of the test, _____ "

(A) the students were tired. (C) the tired students were.

(B) were tired the students? (D) tired were the students.

20. "Do you and your wife have a son?"

"Yes, we do. _____ son is named Patrick, and he lives in Detroit."

(A) His   (C) He

(B) Our   (D) We

Test 35   Articles

Clear Grammar 2, Unit 2

Name _____   Date _____

Part 1   Write *a, an, the,* or — on the lines.

1. *Joe:*   When is the game?

    Mike: Which game do you mean? ___The___ soccer game or ___the___ football game?

    Joe: The football game.

    Mike: Oh! It's on ___X___ Tuesday.

2. *Joan:*   Where is ___the___ apple I put on the table?

    Sue: I put it in ___the___ refrigerator. I didn't know that you needed it now.

3. *April:*   Do you have ___an___ envelope? I need one so I can mail this letter.

    John: No, I don't. But I have ___a___ stamp if you need one.

4. *Ken:*   Does ___the___ sun rise in the west?

    Cara: That's not ___a___ very difficult question.

5. *Jean:*   Would you like ___a___ drink?

    Sean: No, thanks. I'm not thirsty.

6. Yesterday I bought ___a___ cake. We ate ___the___ cake at ___x___ school today.

7. *Jose:*   I can't find ___X___ book that you gave me. Do you know where ___the___ book is?

    Jane: I'm sorry, but I forgot to tell you. I have it.

8. ___X___ Hawaii is located in ___The___ Pacific Ocean.

9. I plan to visit ___X___ Netherlands next year. I really want to see ___X___ Amsterdam.

10. After searching all morning, I finally found ___X___ jacket my brother gave me for
    ___X___ my birthday.

Part 2   Write *a* or *an* on the lines.

1. _____ good book   7. _____ African American

2. _____ helpful person   8. _____ whole apple

3. _____ American   9. _____ cup

4. _____ jet   10. _____ huge pizza

5. _____ uniform   11. _____ telephone

6. _____ very delicious dish   12. _____ hour

Clear Grammar 2, Unit 2

Name _____ Date _____

Part 1 Write *a, an, the,* or — on the lines.

1. *Susan:* Mom, may I borrow _the_ car tonight?

   Mother: Here are _the_ keys, but you will need to put _X_ gas in it.

   Susan: How do you want me to pay for _the_ gas?

   Mother: By credit card or cash. Either is OK:

2. *Bob:* Michael told you where we're going this weekend, right?

   Sami: Yes, he did.

   Bob: Well, what do you think about our plans for _a_ vacation to _a_ foreign country?

   Sami: I think it will be exciting to visit _X_ Mexico, but I'm still studying _the_ Spanish language.

   Bob: I can speak _X_ English as well as _X_ Spanish so I will be all right.

3. *Gina:* I prefer _X_ history to _X_ mathematics. How about you?

   Roberta: Actually, I like _X_ science the best, especially _X_ chemistry. We did _an_ experiment in class yesterday. I made _a_ rocket that actually flew into the air.

4. *Jill:* What types of books do you like to read?

   Miriam: I like to read _X_ fiction, but occasionally I like _X_ exciting real life adventure stories.

   Lindsey: I prefer _X_ biographies.

5. *Joe:* Does anyone live in _the_ house on _the_ corner?

   Peter: No, it's been empty for months. However, the agent has _a_ buyer from _X_ New York.

   Joe: I need to rent _an_ apartment, not buy _a_ house.

Clear Grammar 2

Part 2   Write *a, an, the,* or — on the lines.

1. __The__ month of __✗__ January has __✗__ 31 __✗__ days.

2. The white __✗__ Bengal __✗__ tiger __✗__ cub is __a__ cute __✗__ animal.

3. __✗__ skiing is __✗__ fun to do __✗__ in __the__ winter.

4. I prefer __✗__ to go to __the__ beach __✗__ in __the__ summer.

5. __✗__ my __✗__ favorite __✗__ food is __✗__ pasta with __✗__ tomato and __✗__ meat __✗__ sauce.

6. __✗__ Thanksgiving is __a__ holiday __✗__ when __✗__ many Americans eat __a__ big meal. (*HINT:* It's not the only holiday when this happens.)

7. __✗__ Canada is in __✗__ North __✗__ America __✗__ and __✗__ so is __✗__ Mexico.

8. __✗__ Costa Rica and __✗__ Belize are in __✗__ Central __✗__ America.

9. One of __the__ main __✗__ languages that people speak in __✗__ Algeria is __✗__ Berber.

10. __✗__ jogging is __✗__ one of __the__ most __✗__ popular __✗__ forms of __✗__ exercise.

Part 3   Read each sentence. If the underlined part is correct, circle C. If it is not correct, circle X and write a correction above the sentence.

C   X   1. I prefer <u>to eat sandwich</u> with cheese.

C   X   2. <u>The</u> India is in Asia.

C   X   3. I <u>bought vegetables and milk</u> at the supermarket.

C   X   4. <u>Beach</u> at Siesta Key has very white sand.

C   X   5. <u>Florida</u> is very famous for its oranges.

C   X   6. The pizza <u>at Sergio's</u> is very delicious.

TEST 37 — *Be Going To* + VERBS

Clear Grammar 2, Unit 3

Name _____   Date _____

Part 1   Multiple Choice. Circle the letter of the correct answer.

1. *Andy:*   _____ out dancing this weekend?

    Kanesha: Yes, we are.

    (A)   Are you going go   (C)   You going to go

    (B)   Are you going to go   (D)   Do you go

2. *Katrina:*   _____ to water the plants before we left on vacation?

    Billy: No. I forgot. I hope they are going to be okay.

    (A)   Are you going remember   (C)   Did you remember

    (B)   Are you remember   (D)   Do you remember

3. I usually don't go to concerts, but tonight we _____ my favorite singer!

    (A)   are going to see   (C)   go see

    (B)   are going see   (D)   go to see

4. *Jerry:*   I'm hungry. Can I have a cookie?

    Dad: Don't eat anything! We _____ dinner in five minutes.

    (A)   do have   (C)   are going have

    (B)   did have   (D)   are going to have

5. *Mike:*   I _____ really hard for the test last night.

    Will: Good. Then you should get a good grade.

    (A)   was study   (C)   am going to study

    (B)   studied   (D)   am study

Part 2   Answer the questions below. Use complete sentences and *be + going + to*.

1. What are you going to do tonight?

    _____

2. Are you going to go out this weekend?

    _____

3. What are you going to do at the end of the semester?

    _____

4. Is your family going to visit you here?

    _____

5. When is the class going to study the next chapter in the grammar book?

    _____

Part 3   Circle the error in each sentence. Write a correction on the line.

1. Sara and Richard are going get married next year.   _____

2. We going to go to the museum last night.   _____

3. Do they going to meet their old friends tomorrow?   _____

4. My mother are going to be very mad at me.   _____

5. Where you are going to go on vacation?   _____

Test 38   *Be Going To* + VERBS

Clear Grammar 2, Unit 3

Name _____   Date _____

Part 1   Underline the correct time expression.

1. I study English (right now, every day, tomorrow).

2. They are going to go out to dinner (tonight, every day, last Friday).

3. We visited our grandmother (last month, right now, the day after tomorrow).

4. We are going to leave (last year, tonight, two days ago).

5. She went to Japan (tomorrow, right now, last year).

6. He is watching TV (right now, last year, every day).

7. The teacher (is going to go, is going, goes, went) to Japan every summer.

8. I (going to eat, am eating, eat, ate) ice cream now.

9. They often (are going to visit, are visiting, visit) their grandparents.

10. Cindy and Jan (are going to play, are playing, play, played) at the park yesterday.

11. Joe (is going to be, is being, is, was) in New York next summer.

12. Most of the students in my class this semester (are having, have, had) only one

    brother or sister.

Part 2   Read each sentence. If it is correct, circle C. If it is wrong, circle X and write a correction on the line.

C   X   1. Shirts are going to be on sale yesterday.   _____

C   X   2. Do Joe and Sarah are going to go out tonight?   _____

C   X   3. What we are going to do after dinner?   _____

C   X   4. The final exam for this class is going to be easy.   _____

Clear Grammar 2

Part 3 Write *yes/no* questions based on the sentences below.

1. They are going to go to a concert together.

   Are they going to go to concert togeth

2. Jane is going to attend her class reunion.

   Is Jane going to attend her

3. We are going to do our homework together.

   Are we going to do our hom t

4. You are going to listen to your favorite CD tonight.

   Are you going to - listen to your favor CD t

5. Larry is going to study for a big exam after dinner.

   Is Larry going to

Clear Grammar 2, Units 2 and 3

Name _____   Date _____

Part 1   Write *a, an, the,* or — on the lines.

1. *Jack:*   How many __X__ keys do you have on your __X__ key chain?

   Hank: I think I have six of them.

   Jack: Well, is that confusing? I mean, is it hard to remember which is which?

   Hank: No, not at all. For example, __the__ big one with the red writing is for my

   house, and __the__ smallest key is for my desk at work.

2. When I went shopping, I bought __a__ coat. I'm going to Canada next week, so I'll

   have a chance to wear __the__ coat very soon.

3. __The__ president of __the__ United States is paid over __X__ $400,000 per year.

4. __The__ textbook that we use in this class focuses on __the__ grammar of modern

   English poetry.

5. Can you tell me __The__ main reason that you want to go to __X__ Mexico now?

Part 2   Write *a, an,* or — on the lines.

1. _____ ugly dog		4. _____ umbrellas		7. _____ month		
2. _____ ugly dogs		5. _____ green umbrella		8. _____ hard problem		
3. _____ small ugly dog		6. _____ green umbrellas		9. _____ family reunion		

Part 3   Read each sentence. If it is correct, write C on the line. If it is not correct, write X on the line and write a correction above the sentence.

_____   1.   Jenna going to study with Todd.

_____   2.   Isn't she going to go out tonight?

_____   3.   They not going to help with the class project.

_____   4.   We're going to play tennis together at noon.

_____   5.   They going to fly to San Diego during spring break.

Clear Grammar 2

Part 4 Circle the correct form of each verb.

1. It (is snowing, is going to snow, snows, snowed) in Chicago right now, but the weather here is quite warm.

2. Yesterday Jan and I (are visiting, are going to visit, visit, visited) Ned in the hospital.

3. All of us students (are going to eat, eat, ate) dinner together tonight.

4. If you (are speaking, speak, spoke) English every day, of course your speaking ability will improve a lot.

5. An hour from now, we (are going to play, play, played, playing) football in the park.

Clear Grammar 2

TEST 40   Irregular Past Tense

Clear Grammar 2, Unit 4

Name _____   Date _____

Part 1 Write the correct forms of the verbs on the lines. Pay attention to the verb tense.

1. (speak)   He __spoke__ to Susan a week ago.

2. (lose)   My favorite team __lost__ the game last Sunday.

3. (send)   Jonathan __sent__ some flowers to his grandmother yesterday.

4. (fly)   In winter, the birds in this area __flew__ to South America.

5. (hear)   We __heard__ the news on the radio just now. I was so surprised!

Part 2 Read the story and write the correct forms of the verbs.

I ❶ (get) __get__ up at 6 A.M. almost every day, but this morning

I ❷ (get) __got__ up late. I usually ❸ (eat) __eat__ breakfast,

but I ❹ (have) __had__ no time today. I ❺ (leave) __left__ my

apartment at 9 A.M. and ❻ (drive) __drove__ to work. On the way to

work, I ❼ (hear) __heard__ some noise from my engine, and soon the car

❽ (stop) __stoped__ . I ❾ (know) __knew__ what the problem

❿ (be) __was__ . I ⓫ (call) __called__ a nearby car repair

shop, and a mechanic ⓬ (come) __came__ to look at my car. There

⓭ (be) __were__ two problems with the engine, but he

⓮ (repair) __repaired__ them. It ⓯ (cost) __cost__ me about $200. I

⓰ (arrive) __arrived__ late to work. Today ⓱ (be) __was__ not a

good day for me. I ⓲ (explain) __explained__ the situation to my boss, and she

⓳ (get) __didn't get__ angry at all. She ⓴ (be) __was__ a great boss,

and I ㉑ (like) __like__ her a lot.

Part 3 Answer these questions with complete sentences.

1. Did Mary give him a card?   Yes, _She gave him a card._
2. Did Rick know her last name?   No, _He didn't know her last name._
3. Did you go to the store?   Yes, _I went to the store._
4. Did she find her book bag?   No, _She didn't find her book bag._
5. Did they break the window?   Yes, _They broke the window._
6. Did he become sick?   No, _he didn't become sick._
7. Did the shirt cost a lot?   Yes, _the shirt cost a lot of._
8. Did you take the bus to work?   No, _I didn't take the_

Clear Grammar 2

TEST 41   Irregular Past Tense

Clear Grammar 2, Unit 4

Name _____   Date _____

Part 1   Write the past tense of the verbs on the lines.

1. know _____   7. sing _____
2. find _____   8. fly _____
3. read _____   9. sleep _____
4. eat _____   10. lose _____
5. drink _____   11. come _____
6. meet _____   12. win _____

Part 2   Write the correct forms of the verbs on the lines.

1. (ride)   I ___*rode*___ a big horse last summer.
2. (stand)   We ___*stand*___ for two hours in the rain yesterday trying to get

   tickets.

3. (ring)   They ___*rang*___ our doorbell very late last night, so we didn't

   answer it.

4. (make)   My grandmother ___*made*___ bread every day when she lived in

   France.

5. (shoot)   The hunters ___*shot*___ twenty ducks this morning.
6. (spend)   He ___*spent*___ all his money when he bought his car.
7. (tear)   Maria ___*tore*___ her dress when she fell down.
8. (understand) The test was so easy that we ___*understood*___ it all.

Part 3 Read this paragraph and fill in each blank with the correct form of the verb that is in parentheses.

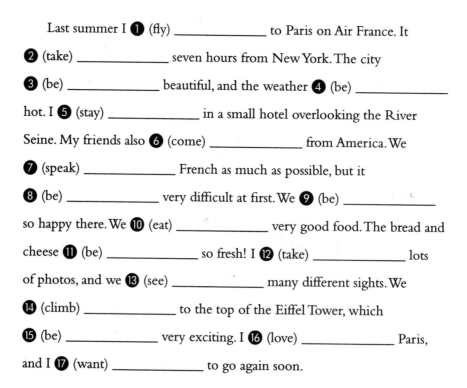

Last summer I ❶ (fly) _____ to Paris on Air France. It

❷ (take) _____ seven hours from New York. The city

❸ (be) _____ beautiful, and the weather ❹ (be) _____

hot. I ❺ (stay) _____ in a small hotel overlooking the River

Seine. My friends also ❻ (come) _____ from America. We

❼ (speak) _____ French as much as possible, but it

❽ (be) _____ very difficult at first. We ❾ (be) _____

so happy there. We ❿ (eat) _____ very good food. The bread and

cheese ⓫ (be) _____ so fresh! I ⓬ (take) _____ lots

of photos, and we ⓭ (see) _____ many different sights. We

⓮ (climb) _____ to the top of the Eiffel Tower, which

⓯ (be) _____ very exciting. I ⓰ (love) _____ Paris,

and I ⓱ (want) _____ to go again soon.

TEST 42   Verb Tenses

Clear Grammar 1, Units 1, 2, 5, 6, and 9
Clear Grammar 2, Units 3 and 4

Name _____   Date _____

Part 1   Write the correct forms of the verbs on the lines. Pay attention to the verb tense.

1. (assist)   He _____ assisted _____ the teacher in the computer lab yesterday.

2. (go)   The students _____ are going to _____ play soccer tomorrow.

3. (cut)   Jose _____ cut _____ himself while he was shaving two days ago.

4. (eat)   They _____ eate _____ too much during the last Christmas vacation.

5. (be)   We thought we _____ were _____ ready for the exam, but we didn't do well.

6. (drive)   He _____ drives _____ to school every day, doesn't he?

7. (love)   Tina _____ loves _____ Mike very much now.

8. (be)   Lucy and I _____ were _____ students at the same university five years ago.

9. (cry)   She _____ cried _____ when she heard the sad news yesterday.

10. (make)   Taro _____ is making _____ tea for us now.

Part 2 Read the story. Choose verbs from the box to fill in the blanks. Be sure to use the correct form of each verb.

be	have	go	come	see	cost	pay	leave	enjoy

I like to ❶ _____go_____ to the movies on

weekends. It usually ❷ _____~~costs~~_____ me only four dollars

because I ❸ _____have_____ a student ID now. Yesterday

I ❹ _____went_____ to a very cheap theater. It only

❺ _____cost_____ me a dollar. Yes, I only

❻ _____paid_____ one dollar. There

❼ _____~~had~~ were_____ a lot of people in the theater.

When I go to the movies, I always ❽ _____~~see~~ enjoy_____

the previews. (Previews are the advertisements of the movies that

❾ _____are coming to_____ the theater very soon.) I enjoyed the

movie and ❿ _____~~come~~ left_____ the theater at 10 P.M. I

⓫ _____~~enjoy am coming~~ to see_____ another movie next weekend. I can't wait

till then!

TEST 43   Verb Tenses

Clear Grammar 1, Units 1, 2, 5, 6, and 9
Clear Grammar 2, Units 3 and 4

Name _____   Date _____

Part 1   Multiple Choice. Circle the letter of the correct answer.

1. *Jack:*   Where _____ Will and Cassandra _____ ?

    Sam: To the beach. If they drive quickly, they will get there by 10 A.M.

    (A)   do . . . go   (C)   are . . . going

    (B)   are . . . go   (D)   is . . . going

2. *Bob:*   What's this red stuff on my chicken?

    Lisa: It's paprika. Hungarian people commonly _____ paprika as a spice.

    (A)   use   (C)   are use

    (B)   using   (D)   uses

3. *April:*   Listen! Why _____ those dogs _____ ?

    Mike: Maybe they are nervous about something.

    (A)   is . . . bark   (C)   do . . . bark

    (B)   are . . . bark   (D)   are . . . barking

4. *Joseph:*   Is Gertrude a German language teacher?

    Michelle: Yes, but she _____ French last year.

    (A)   teached   (C)   teach

    (B)   is teaching   (D)   taught

5. *George:*   _____ you _____ to Rachel's party last night?

    Ned: No, I worked till midnight.

    (A)   Do . . . go   (C)   Were . . . go

    (B)   Did . . . go   (D)   Are . . . go

Part 2 Read the story and write the correct forms of the verbs.

Dear Mom,

Thank you for your last letter. I **1** (receive)

_____ it yesterday after school.

Right now I **2** (take) _____ a break

from my studies, so I **3** (have) _____

a few minutes to write you a short letter. Everything here

4 (be) _____ fine. My classmates and I

5 (be) _____ very busy with school-

work. As you know, final exams **6** (come) _____

_____ soon, so we **7** (study) _____

every night this week at the library until it

8 (close) _____ at midnight. Before

I forget, I **9** (have) _____ some

bad news. **10** (remember) _____ you

_____ my friend Bill? Well, he

11 (have) _____ a pretty bad car

accident last month. He **12** (stay) _____

in the hospital for two weeks, so he **13** (go, neg) _____

_____ to school during that time. The university

14 (tell) _____ him to take the rest

of the semester off. He **15** (come) _____

_____ back next semester. Well, I **16** (have, neg)

_____ time to write more. I just

17 (want) _____ to tell you that I love

you and miss you! Please write back soon.

Your son,

Herve

TEST 44 Verb Tenses

Clear Grammar 1, **Units 1, 2, 5, 6, and 9**
Clear Grammar 2, **Units 3 and 4**

Name _____ Date _____

Part 1 Fill in each blank using the subject and verb that are in parentheses. Be sure to use the correct verb tense.

Phil: Hey, Vic. How ❶ (be / you) _____ ?

Vic: ❷ (I / do) _____ OK.

Phil: ❸ (I / have) _____ something to ask you.

Vic: Sure. What ❹ (you / want) _____ to know?

Phil: What ❺ (you / do) _____ next Saturday?

Vic: ❻ (I / not / know) _____ . Why?

Phil: ❼ (I / go) _____ to Nedra's house last night.

❽ (we / decide) _____ to go to the park.

❾ (you / want) _____ to go with us?

Vic: ❿ (many people / go) _____ there on the weekend?

Phil: ⓫ (I / not / be) _____ sure.

Vic: When was the last time that ⓬ (you and Nedra / have) _____

_had____ a picnic there?

Phil: About three weeks ago. ⓭ (it / be) _____ on a Saturday.

Vic: Well, ⓮ (there / be) _____ many people there?

Phil: No, not really. ⓯ (we / have) _____ a great time, and

that's why ⓰ (we / want) _____ to go there again.

Vic: OK. ⓱ (it / sound) _____ good to me. I think that

⓲ (I / go) _____ with you and Nedra next Saturday.

Part 2 Read each sentence. If the underlined verb is correct, write C on the line. If it is not correct, write X on the line and write a correction above the verb mistake.

_____ 1. We <u>are going to go</u> to the zoo tomorrow.

_____ 2. I <u>didn't had</u> a good feeling after I finished that job interview.

_____ 3. All of the clerks <u>are attending</u> a sales meeting right now.

_____ 4. She took the prices off the gifts, and then she <u>wrap</u> them with colorful paper.

_____ 5. Chung doesn't get to class on time because he <u>woke</u> up late.

TEST 45   *How* Questions

Clear Grammar 2, Unit 5

Name _____   Date _____

Part 1   Underline the correct words in these conversations.

1. Q: How (much, many, often) time do you spend working in your yard every week?

    A: About two hours.

2. Q: How (tall, long, short) is the Statue of Liberty?

    A: It is 152 feet and 2 inches.

3. Q: How (long, often, many) does the teacher give a test?

    A: She gives one once a week.

4. Q: How (far, long, much) away from school do you live?

    A: My apartment is only two miles away.

5. Q: How (many, often, old) is your watch?

    A: My father bought it for me, so I am not sure, but it's made of gold.

Part 2   Write a *how* question for each of these sentences. Use the words in italics to help you write the correct question.

1. Michael and Kim jogged *five miles* this morning.

    _____

2. It took *17 years* to build the Taj Mahal.

    How many years did it take to build the Taj maha

3. Mount Everest is *8,848 meters* tall.

    How tall is the Mon Ev. ?

4. Mom needs *two cups of* sugar to make Lisa's birthday cake.

    How many caps Does mom need to mule kis, cah

5. The chess club meets *once a week*.

    How often does ches club meet ?

Part 3 Underline the error in each sentence. Write a correction on the line.

1. How often you go to the beach? _____

2. What angry was your dad when you told him
   him about the accident? _____

3. How long is it to the grocery store from here? _____

4. How much brothers and sisters do you have? _____

5. How high is Michael Jordan? _____

Clear Grammar 2

Clear Grammar 2, Unit 5

Name _____   Date _____

Part 1   Fill in the blanks with the correct words.

1.   Q: How _____ did that CD cost you?

     A: $15.00.

2.   Q: How _____ was she in the hospital?

     A: Three days in total.

3.   Q: How _____ is your sister?

     A: She's 5'5".

4.   Q: How _____ is the school from here?

     A: About three miles.

5.   Q: How _____ students are there at your English language school?

     A: I think we have around 100 students.

6.   Q: How _____ does the wrestler weigh?

     A: I would say at least 200 pounds.

7.   Q: How _____ is that student?

     A: I don't know, but she looks too young to be a college student.

8.   Q: How _____ do you go to the library each week?

     A: Almost every day.

9.   Q: How _____ is your apartment?

     A: Well, there are three bedrooms. It's a good size.

10. Q: How _____ did it take you to get here?

     A: It took us about three hours.

Clear Grammar 2

Part 2 Write a *how* question for each of these sentences.

1. The puppy is only three months old.

   _____

2. Kent weighs only 130 pounds.

   _____

3. Lin studied English every day in high school.

   _____

4. Matt is 5'11".

   _____

5. It's about 20 miles to the next town.

   _____

6. There are 2.2 pounds in a kilo.

   _____

7. There are 100 tests in this textbook.

   _____

8. They dated for two years before they got married.

   _____

9. The mall was very crowded before the holidays.

   _____

10. I usually drive 60 miles per hour.

    _____

Clear Grammar 2

Clear Grammar 2, Units 4 and 5

Name _____   Date _____

Part 1   Write the past tense of the verbs on the lines.

1. become   _____   11. see   _____

2. bring   _____   12. make   _____

3. mean   _____   13. build   _____

4. run   _____   14. blow   _____

5. come   _____   15. buy   _____

6. read   _____   16. choose   _____

7. throw   _____   17. wear   _____

8. tell   _____   18. win   _____

9. shut   _____   19. spread   _____

10. put   _____   20. fly   _____

Part 2   Read this short paragraph and fill in the correct forms of the verbs.

I live near the Everglades in southern Florida. What a beautiful

place it is! Yesterday I (go) ❶ _____ fishing.

I (see) ❷ _____ many strange birds feeding at the

lake. There (be) ❸ _____ an alligator on the bank

in the sun. The sky (be) ❹ _____ blue, and the

sunshine on my face (feel) ❺ _____ good. After

lunch I (close) ❻ _____ my eyes and

(fall) ❼ _____ asleep. I

(sleep) ❽ _____ for only a short time. Then my

fishing pole (move) ❾ _____ suddenly. I

(have) ❿ _____ a fish on my line, but it

(swim) ⓫ _____ away before I could reel it in.

Clear Grammar 2

1. *A:* How _____ is your swimming pool?

    B: 6.6 feet at the deep end.

2. *A:* How _____ does that package weigh?

    B: 10 pounds.

3. *A:* How _____ is it to Nashville from here?

    B: 17 miles.

4. *A:* How _____ is your grandfather?

    B: He's 87.

5. *A:* How _____ do you work out?

    B: Three times a week.

6. *A:* How _____ can you run?

    B: 3 miles without stopping.

7. *A:* How _____ people can sleep in your tent?

    B: 4.

8. *A:* How _____ rice did you cook?

    B: 3 cups.

TEST 48   Adverbs of Frequency

Clear Grammar 2, Unit 6

Name _____   Date _____

Part 1   Match the adverb of frequency on the left with the phrase on the right that has the same meaning.

1. _____ rarely   A.   some of the time

2. _____ always   B.   much of the time

3. _____ often   C.   not at any time

4. _____ never   D   almost never

5. _____ usually   E.   most of the time

6. _____ sometimes   F.   all of the time

Part 2   Rewrite the following sentences using an adverb of frequency.

1. The students study in the library all of the time.

   The students always study in the library.

2. I am happy all of the time.

   I am always happy

3. The teacher is almost never in her office after class.

   The teacher is rarely in her office after class.

4. You will find Jun at his favorite coffee shop most of the time.

   You will usually find Jun at his favorite coffee shop.

Part 3   Correct the errors in these sentences.

1. The students do always their homework on time.

   The student always do their homework on time

2. You do study how often?

   How often do you study?

3. What time are you go usually to the store?

   What time are you usually go to the store?

4. The grammar teacher have always a book or paper in her hand.

   The grammar teacher always have a book or p

TEST 49 Adverbs of Frequency

Clear Grammar 2, Unit 6

Name _____   Date _____

Part 1   Write new sentences using an adverb of frequency.

1. My dog likes to eat all of the time.

   _My dog always likes to eat_____

2. On the weekends, we go to the movies most of the time.

   _On the weekends we usually go to the movies_____

3. Rob and Peter almost never go to bed before midnight.

   _Rob and Peter rarely go to bed before midnight_____

4. Much of the time I don't eat breakfast. I have just a cup of coffee most of the time.

   Oftenly I don't eat breakfast. I usually have just a cup of coffee

5. My neighbors almost never use their swimming pool. It is empty most of the time.

   My neighbors rarely use their swimming pool. It is usually empty

6. On Sunday mornings, I wash my car most of the time.

   _On Sunday mornings, I usually wash my car._____

7. Mary and Louise don't do their English homework at any time!

   _Mary and Louise never do their English homework._____

Part 2   Fill in each blank with the correct adverb of frequency.

1. _____ not at any time

2. _____ all of the time

3. _____ some of the time

4. _____ most of the time

5. _____ almost never

6. _____ much of the time

7. _____ almost never

Part 3 Underline the correct forms.

1. The children (take usually, usually take) their lunch to school.

2. I (always read, read always) the cartoons first when I read the newspaper.

3. Hurricanes (usually occur, occur usually) in the summertime.

4. I (go never, never go) jogging before breakfast.

5. My computer teacher (seldom gives, gives seldom) homework.

6. People (fail rarely, rarely fail) the driving test because it is easy.

7. The students (practice sometimes, sometimes practice) on the golf course.

8. Flights from San Francisco (often are, are often) delayed due to the weather.

9. Peter and Marc (rollerblade usually, usually rollerblade) to school.

10. I (never can, can never) understand Mr. Choi. He speaks with a heavy accent.

TEST 50   Object Pronouns

Clear Grammar 2, Unit 7

Name _____   Date _____

Part 1   Underline the correct form of each pronoun or adjective.

1. Please give this book to (she, her).

2. (We, Our) luggage was not on the plane.

3. I went to the concert with (me, my) girlfriend.

4. Brian works at a bank. (He, Him) likes to work there.

5. (I, My) parents love (I, me) very much.

6. Roberto has a wonderful accent. I love to hear (him, he) speak.

7. My brother and his friends like to play soccer. (They, Them) are very good players.

8. My husband and I bought a new car. (We, Our) like (it, its) very much.

Part 2   Write the correct form of each pronoun or adjective.

1. Our apartment is very dirty. _____ are going to clean _____ today.

2. My mom asked my sister to go to the store. _____ wants _____ to buy some milk.

3. We were absent this morning. Did Ms. Cooper give _____ class homework?

4. John forgot to bring _____ book to class. _____ couldn't do any of the exercises.

5. Anna wants to bring _____ friend to the party. Is it okay?

6. The boys threw a rock at the window. _____ damaged _____ very badly.

Part 3   Circle the error in each sentence. Write a correction on the line.

1. Does her want to meet the new teacher? _____

2. Kevin went with we to the theater. _____

3. They live near I. _____

4. They need to buy he a birthday present. _____

5. Me don't like to play games. _____

TEST 51 Object Pronouns

Clear Grammar 2, Unit 7

Name _____   Date _____

Part 1   In each blank on the left, write the correct letter of the matching object pronoun.

Subject Pronouns	Object Pronouns
_____ 1. they	A. me
_____ 2. she	B. him
_____ 3. I	C. you
_____ 4. it	D. them
_____ 5. he	E. us
_____ 6. we	F. her
_____ 7. you	G. it

Part 2   Underline the correct pronouns.

1. It is important to give (they, them) the correct change.

2. I have to telephone (her, she) tonight before 10:00 P.M.

3. That package is for (we, us), not for (they, them).

4. The house at the end of the street belongs to (she, her).

5. Jane is coming to see (I, me) this afternoon.

6. Mary's dog is a poodle. She never takes (it, its) for a walk.

7. We visit our family in Louisiana every Thanksgiving. We usually visit (they, them) for

    a week.

8. Please call the office and give (they, them) your fax number.

9. John called and left a message for you to call (he, him) back.

10. That order is for (I, me). The other one is for (her, she).

Clear Grammar 2

Part 3   Read each sentence. If the underlined part is correct, circle C. If it is not correct, circle X and write a correction above it.

C   X   1.   Megan gave <u>her</u> book to Chris for the weekend.

C   X   2.   Jamie and Marco gave <u>we</u> a ride home after the party.

C   X   3.   The teacher told <u>he</u> to go to the office after class.

C   X   4.   Jane's father gave <u>her</u> a computer for her birthday.

C   X   5.   The wind blew <u>they</u> off course in their boat.

C   X   6.   The fruit is very cheap now, so <u>we</u> will buy a lot.

C   X   7.   The police officer gave <u>me</u> a ticket for speeding.

C   X   8.   My brother called me for some information, so I gave it to <u>he</u>.

TEST 52   Review

Clear Grammar 2, Units 6 and 7

Name _____   Date _____

Part 1   Each sentence has two blanks. Fill in *one* of the blanks with the correct adverb of frequency: *always, usually, often, sometimes, rarely, never,* or *ever.* Do not write anything in the other blank in the sentence.

1.   I play tennis seven days a week. I _____ play _____ every day.

2.   We only drink champagne on New Year's Eve, so I _____ drink

    _____ it.

3.   The bus stops here every hour on the hour. It _____ is _____ on

    time, so don't be late.

4.   The desert is very dry because there is very little rain. It _____ rains

    _____ in the desert.

5.   Some vegetarians only eat vegetables and fruit. They _____ eat

    _____ meat or fish.

6.   Other vegetarians will eat a little white meat from time to time. They _____

    eat _____ chicken or fish.

7.   Peter studies hard for his tests and gets good grades. He _____ makes

    _____ an A.

8.   In the monsoon season in India it rains heavily every day. It _____ rains

    _____ during the monsoon season.

9.   Lorna _____ gets _____ to work at 8 A.M., but for the past two

    days she has been late. This is really odd!

Part 2 Underline the correct form of each pronoun or adjective.

1. This package is for (our, we, us).

2. (Me, My, I) classes begin on Monday.

3. (He, Him) is a very clever computer programmer.

4. Do (you, your) go to the movies often?

5. (Them, They, Their) will be going to the soccer match in Orlando on Saturday.

6. (She, Her) has lost 30 pounds in weight since she started running.

7. That dog is very naughty. (Its, It) does not obey anyone.

8. (Me, My, I) dream is to win the lottery.

Part 3 Read this passage. There are nine mistakes. Circle the mistakes and write the correct form above each mistake.

Yesterday all of me family went to the beach. We took a picnic lunch with us. We found a nice place to sit by the water. My son and her friend brought us sail boat, and they went out in him. It was very windy, so they had a good time. My wife and me sat on us chairs in the sun and read our books. We brought sandwiches to eat. It was good. My daughter Juliet didn't bring a friend. Her was alone, so her was bored. I built her a sand castle later on, and then we all went swimming. There were many fish in the water.

Clear Grammar 2

TEST 53 One and Other

Clear Grammar 2, Unit 8

Name _____   Date _____

Part 1   Multiple Choice. Circle the letter of the correct answer.

1. *Lynn:*   Do you have a pen?

   Wes: I think there is _____ in my desk.

   (A)   it   (C)   some

   (B)   one   (D)   other

2. Bob has three cars. Two of them are blue, and _____ is red.

   (A)   two   (C)   the other

   (B)   it   (D)   another

3. I need to buy three birthday presents for my mom. I bought one yesterday. I have to

   buy _____ today. Her party is tonight.

   (A)   the other one   (C)   the others

   (B)   the others ones   (D)   another one

4. *Patty:*   Susan can't find her grammar book.

   Bud: I think _____ is in her bedroom.

   (A)   it   (C)   some

   (B)   one   (D)   others

5. *Tim:*   We need five apples for dessert. Are there five in the refrigerator?

   Tina: No, only four. We'll need to get _____ at the grocery store.

   (A)   other one   (C)   another one

   (B)   the others one   (D)   anothers

Part 2 Read these sentences. Fill in the blanks with these words: *one, it, other, another, others, the other,* or *the others.*

1. This shirt is dirty. I need to put on _____ one before we leave.

2. This grocery store is closed. Don't worry. _____ are open.

3. My brother has two children. One is named Rachel, and _____ is named William.

4. We need a spoon to stir this soup. Do you have _____ ?

5. My purse is in the living room. Can you get _____ for me?

6. The classroom is very crowded. Five students are studying. Four students are writing papers. _____ are listening to the teacher.

7. Some people arrived at 7:00 P.M. _____ arrived at 9:00 P.M.

8. Can I have _____ sheet of paper? I made a mistake on this one.

9. Art wants that piece of chocolate. Please give _____ to him.

10. This computer isn't working. We're going to have to use _____ .

Part 3 Circle the error in each sentence. Write a correction above the sentence.

1. This book looks interesting, so I might buy one.

2. Lions and bears are mammals. A monkey is other example.

3. Bob wants that apple. Please give one to him.

4. My sons are Jim and Bob. One is in Florida, and another is in Texas.

5. Blue is a good color for a shirt. White is other.

TEST 54 *One* and *Other*

Clear Grammar 2, Unit 8

Name _____   Date _____

Part 1   Fill in the blanks with one of these words: *one, it, other, another, others, the other,* and *the others.*

A few days ago, I went to visit my grandmother. On the way, I stopped at a

bakery to buy her some chocolate chip cookies. They are her favorite. Since the

bakery was out of chocolate chip cookies, I went to ❶ _____ . This

bakery had chocolate chip cookies, and the woman behind the counter gave me

❷ _____ to taste. ❸ _____ was so good that I decided to

buy some for myself, too.

After leaving the bakery, I was feeling tired, so I decided to take a taxi the

rest of the way to grandmother's house. I waved at a taxi as ❹ _____

passed by, but the driver didn't see me. So I walked to the other corner, where

two taxis were parked. I asked ❺ _____ driver if he would take me,

but he said he was waiting for a passenger. Then, I asked ❻ _____

driver. However, she was off duty, and I ended up walking to my grandmother's

house. When I arrived there, Grandmother wasn't even home!

Part 2   Read each sentence. If the underlined part is correct, write C on the line. If the underlined part is not correct, write X on the line and write a correction above the error.

_____ 1. I had three pieces of candy. I ate two and gave <u>another one</u> to my friend.

_____ 2. Some people like fish. <u>Another</u> people like different kinds of seafood.

_____ 3. To me, choosing a car involves two things. One is cost, and <u>the other</u> is

comfort.

_____ 4. Our Mazda is a small red car. Our <u>another</u> car is a dark gray Toyota.

_____ 5. I have one cat, and she is enough. I don't want <u>other</u>.

Part 3 Write *another, the other, it, one, others,* or *the others* on the lines. In some cases, more than one answer is possible.

1. That was a great hamburger! I think I'll have _____ .

2. *A:* Where is my math book?

   B: Isn't _____ on the kitchen table with your _____ books?

3. *A:* Which TV show do you want to watch? This one?

   B: No, I want to watch the _____ you had on earlier.

4. I found one of my shoes but not _____ .

5. I don't like these gloves. Do you have _____ that I can try on?

TEST 55   Possessive

Clear Grammar 2, Unit 9

Name _____   Date _____

Part 1   Multiple Choice. Circle the letter of the correct answer.

1. *Jackie:* _____ pencil is this?

    Marv: It's Bob's.

    (A) Who   (C) Whom

    (B) Whose   (D) What

2. _____ is very messy.

    (A) The top the table   (C) The top of the table

    (B) The table's top   (D) The top of the table's

3. *Hank:* _____ ?

    Fran: I think it is April's.

    (A) Whose hat is that   (C) Who is that hat

    (B) Whose is that hat   (D) Who that hat is

4. Andrew is _____ husband.

    (A) hers   (C) she

    (B) her   (D) her's

5. This is _____ newspaper.

    (A) yesterdays   (C) yesterday's

    (B) of yesterday   (D) the yesterday's

Part 2   Combine each pair of sentences to make a new sentence. Use the correct possessive form.

1. Michael has a dog. It is black and white.

    Michael's dog is black & white.

2. Mr. Erb owns a house. It is very big.

    Mr Erb's house is very big house.

3. Laura has a hobby. It is stamp collecting.

    Laura's hobby is stamp collecting.

Clear Grammar 2

4. The mail is from Japan. The mail belongs to Rachel.

   The mail is from Japan as Rachel's

5. The bird has a nest. It is high in the oak tree.

   The bird's nest is high in the oak tree

Part 3 Read this short passage. Circle the mistakes and write the correct forms above the mistakes. There are 3 mistakes. (*Hint:* Check possessive forms.)

This magazine is very interesting. The name of the magazine is *Egyptian Adventures.* It is about the history of Egypt.

I bought this magazine at the bookstore on Forest Avenue. The magazine's price is $7. I think this magazine is a little expensive. The price of the magazine needs to be cheaper.

Egyptian Adventures is printed by Adventure Publishers. This is not the only magazine of Adventure Publishers. They print another famous magazine. That magazine's name is *World Events.* The information in this magazine is very important for history teachers.

Adventure Publisher's magazines are very interesting. I hope you will read one of them in the future.

TEST 56 Possessive

Clear Grammar 2, Unit 9

Name _____   Date _____

Part 1 Write the corresponding subject pronouns on the lines.

1. _____ my   4. _____ their

2. _____ his   5. _____ our

3. _____ your   6. _____ her

Part 2 Fill in the blanks with a possessive adjective.

When I was in Japan last year, I wanted to climb Mount Fuji. Since I forgot

to bring ❶ _____ hiking shoes, I borrowed a pair from my friend

Tim. Unfortunately, ❷ _____ shoes were too big, so I had to buy a

pair of ❸ _____ own shoes. Then, someone told me that I should

wear a hat. Since I did not have a hat with me either, I asked another friend. He

didn't have a hat, but his sister did, and he said I could borrow ❹ _____

hat. I wanted to, but the hat was too big, so I had to buy ❺ _____

own. When I went to buy a hat, I also bought a pair of long pants, some gloves,

and a flashlight. Then, I realized that I did not have enough money to buy a

train ticket to Mount Fuji. I was still able to go, though, because some friends

who had a car told me they wanted to go. I told them that if we could use

❻ _____ car, we could go together.

Part 3 Circle the correct possessive forms.

1. The <u>movie's end / end of the movie</u> was disappointing.

2. I found this wallet at the airport, but I don't know <u>whose / who's</u> it is.

3. The <u>car of the basketball player / basketball player's car</u> was very expensive.

4. Is this <u>their / theirs</u> disk or <u>mines / mine</u>?

5. *Alice:* Since it's raining out, can I borrow <u>your / yours</u> umbrella?

   Bill: <u>My / Mine's / Mine</u> is broken, but here's my <u>sister / sister's</u>. You can use

   <u>her's / hers</u>.

6. <u>Whose / who's</u> turn is it to drive?

7. That's not my pencil. It's <u>her's / hers</u>.

Clear Grammar 2, Units 8 and 9

Name _____ Date _____

Part 1 Write *one, it, another, other, the other,* or *the others* on the line as appropriate.

1. *Steve:* Where's the key to the house?

   Mike: I don't know. I thought you had _____ !

2. *Bob:* Remember to call your friends from class about the camping trip.

   Rick: I will. And you will call our _____ friends, right?

3. *Janet:* What's in the bag?

   Ted: Philadelphia soft pretzels. Would you like _____ ?

4. *Sue:* Which sweater do you like, this blue one or this red one?

   Gina: I don't like either of them. Why don't you choose _____ ?

5. *Tony:* Do you remember Dr. Tan from U.S. history class last semester?

   Joe: Yes, of course. I think he's teaching _____ course on American history.

6. *Ken:* I visited Japan, Korea, and Hong Kong while I was in the military.

   Ann: Really? Did you visit any _____ countries during that time?

Part 2 Write the correct possessive forms in the blanks.

1. *Teacher:* Does anyone know _____ book this is?

   Student: I think it's Rod's. He called me last night and told me he lost his book.

2. *Clerk:* Is that your purse, miss?

   Customer: No, it's not _____ . Maybe you should ask the woman standing

   over there. Perhaps it's _____ .

3. *Jack:* I'll meet you at my friends' house.

   Tina: I'd rather we go together because I don't know where _____

   house is.

Clear Grammar 2

Part 3 Read each sentence. If it is correct, write C on the line. If it is not correct, write X on the line and write a correction above the sentence.

_____ 1. The car's price is $10,000.

_____ 2. The cake is on the table's top.

_____ 3. I don't know whose wallet this is.

_____ 4. I don't know who's going to go to the picnic.

_____ 5. Are those your floppy disks or are they mines?

_____ 6. I think this house is the professor's. He's very rich.

_____ 7. The hotel's name is Country Inn.

_____ 8. My dogs name is Cuddles.

TEST 58 Comparative and Superlative

Clear Grammar 2, Unit 10

Name _____   Date _____

Part 1   Look at the chart. Then complete the following sentences with the correct form of the verb in parentheses. Use the comparative or superlative form. Be sure to add *than* with comparative forms.

Potter's Garden Center Rose Information Chart

Roses	Color	Flower Size	Stem Length	Popularity
Charlie Chaplin	light red	3 inches	9 inches	10 bushes sold this year
American Beauty	medium red	5 inches	10 inches	45 bushes sold this year
Passion	dark red	4 inches	12 inches	60 bushes sold this year

1.   All the roses are red. However, the American Beauty rose is _____ (dark) the Chaplin.

2.   The Passion rose is _____ (dark) rose of all.

3.   The flower of the Chaplin rose is _____ (small) the flower of the American Beauty rose.

4.   The flower of the American Beauty rose is _____ (big) of all.

5.   The Chaplin rose has _____ (short) stem.

6.   The American Beauty's stem is _____ (long) the Chaplin's stem.

7.   This year the store sold _____ (few) Chaplain roses than Passion roses.

8.   The Chaplin rose is _____ (popular) the American beauty.

9.   The Passion rose is _____ (popular) of all.

Part 2 Look at the chart. Then complete the sentences with the correct form of the word in parentheses. Use the comparative or superlative form. Be sure to add *than* with comparative forms.

Daytona Speedway Racing Statistics

Car Number	Average Speed	Distance	Pit Stops★
Car 1	125 mph★★	4 laps★★★	2
Car 2	145 mph	6 laps	1
Car 3	160 mph	9 laps	3

★ A *pit stop* is a break in a race when the race car gets new tires and its engine is checked.
★★ mph = **m**iles **p**er **h**our.
★★★A *lap* is one time around the race track.

1. Car 1 was _____ (slow) Car 2.

2. Car 3 was _____ (fast) car of all.

3. In speed, Car 1 did _____ (bad) of all.

4. Car 2 went _____ (far) Car 1.

5. Car 3 went _____ (far) of all the racers.

6. Car 2 only made 6 laps, but Car 1 made _____ (few) laps of all.

7. Car 2 stopped _____ (less) Car 3.

8. Car 2 stopped _____ (less) of all the racers.

9. Overall, Car 3 was _____ (good) racer of all.

Clear Grammar 2

TEST 59 Comparative and Superlative

Clear Grammar 2, Unit 10

Name _____   Date _____

Part 1 Write the comparative or superlative forms of the words in parentheses on the lines.

1. I am _____ (tall) than my brother Mike.

2. This is _____ (interesting) book we have ever read.

3. Sarah's cakes are good, but Jane's are _____ (good).

4. Some people get better grades because they study hard. Others get better grades because they are _____ (intelligent).

5. If you don't find a _____ (fast) way to get there, we are going to be late.

Part 2 Read each sentence. If it is correct, write C on the line. If it is not correct, write X on the line and write a correction above the sentence.

_____ 1. This is a more easier way of solving that math problem.

_____ 2. Your sister's room is cleaner than yours.

_____ 3. Mr. Jones is the most nicest teacher in the school.

_____ 4. Parents are usually more wise than their children.

_____ 5. I like this chair best because it is the comfortablest.

Part 3   Write the comparative and superlative forms of the following list of words on the lines.

		Comparative	Superlative
1.	delicious	_____	_____
2.	bad	_____	_____
3.	tired	_____	_____
4.	pleasant	_____	_____
5.	far	_____	_____

Part 4   Fill in the blanks with a comparative or superlative form.

The other day I went shopping with my sister. What a frustrating experience! First, we stopped at a clothing store, where my sister tried on a pair of gloves. Since they were too big, my sister asked the clerk if he had a ❶ _____ pair. He did, but they were in a different color, so we went to another store. At that store, my sister found the gloves in the size and color she liked, but they were ❷ _____ than in the first store. When she asked the clerk why they were so expensive, he be- came angry, so we left. Since I was sick of shopping by that point, I took my sister to ❸ _____ clothing store I could find. It was huge. In fact, when I first walked in the store, I couldn't believe the size of this store! My sister finally found a pair that she liked and could afford, but then she decided that she really didn't need to buy a pair of gloves.

Clear Grammar 2, Unit 11

Name _____   Date _____

Part 1   Multiple Choice. Circle the letter of the correct answer.

1. Clerks at fast-food restaurants often say, "_____ I help you?"

   (A) Will   (C) May

   (B) Must   (D) Would

2. Excuse me. _____ you pass me the salt?

   (A) Shall   (C) Must

   (B) Will   (D) Should

3. This cake is too sweet. It _____ have so much sugar in it.

   (A) wouldn't   (C) couldn't

   (B) didn't   (D) shouldn't

4. Do you have plans for the holidays? What _____ do on New Year's Eve?

   (A) will   (C) shall you

   (B) would you   (D) are you going to

5. I turned the heat on half an hour ago, but it's still cold in here. It _____ be warm

   in here by now.

   (A) has to   (C) should

   (B) is going to   (D) would

6. When _____ you like to go shopping? Any time is OK with me.

   (A) may   (C) can

   (B) had better   (D) would

7. I'm cold. _____ you close the window, please?

   (A) Might   (C) Will

   (B) May   (D) Should

8. Masako is her name, and she speaks Japanese perfectly. She _____ be Japanese.

    (A)   will   (C)   would

    (B)   must   (D)   ought

9. _____ you do me a favor? How can I save this file in the computer?

    (A)   Should   (C)   May

    (B)   Would   (D)   Must

10. We _____ clean the room now. Mommy and Daddy are coming home soon.

    (A)   can   (C)   going to

    (B)   could   (D)   had better

Part 2   Underline the correct modals in this conversation about a special dinner celebration.

A: Tomorrow is your birthday. I'd like to take you out for dinner.

B: Another birthday? I ❶ (shouldn't, can't, wouldn't) believe I ❷ (will, can, might) be thirty.

A: Where ❸ (could, will, would) you like to go? I want to take you out to dinner at a really nice restaurant for your birthday.

B: No, you ❹ (wouldn't, shouldn't, couldn't) do that. It's not necessary.

A: Yes, I would really like to. ❺ (Would, Could, Might) you like to go to the Thai restaurant that we went to before?

B: Yes, that sounds really nice. But tomorrow is Friday, so there ❻ (had better, must have, might) be a lot of people there. We ❼ (can, must, may) have to wait for a long time.

A: Don't worry. I know a friend who works there. I ❽ (will, am going, should) to ask him to reserve a table for us.

B: Really, that ❾ (can, must, would) be wonderful.

A: Don't eat too much for lunch tomorrow. You ❿ (may, had better, can) be hungry for a big dinner.

TEST 61 Modals

Clear Grammar 2, Unit 11

Name _____   Date _____

Part 1   Circle the correct modal form.

1.   If you want to do well on the English test tomorrow, you <u>might /should</u> study.

2.   This watch <u>should / must</u> be Jim's. He said he lost his watch here yesterday.

3.   I still don't know what I'm going to do this weekend. I <u>must / had better / might</u> go to the beach.

4.   Ken <u>will / would</u> return to Japan next summer.

5.   Last month my house was robbed twice. You <u>can / had better</u> lock your back door, too.

Part 2   Complete the sentences and questions by writing the modal in parentheses on the correct line.

1.   _____ I _____ use your phone to call my roommate? (may)

2.   Where _____ we _____ buy tickets to the concert? (can)

3.   When _____ they _____ begin the test? (should)

4.   How _____ Ann _____ get in touch with you? (can)

Part 3   Read each sentence. If it is correct, write C on the line. If it is not correct, write X on the line and write a correction above the sentence.

_____   1.   Can you speak Japanese?

_____   2.   He may leaves early because his class will begin at 8 A.M.

_____   3.   They may not come to the party because they had better study for a test.

_____   4.   She wants to see that movie, but she can't. She has to pack for her business trip.

_____   5.   If I were rich, I would travel to Europe and Asia.

_____   6.   Some of my friends might not to go to the party.

_____   7.   That knife isn't very sharp. You ought use another one.

_____   8.   If you want to win the tennis tournament next month, you'd better practice more often.

_____   9.   Last month we must buy more firewood because the weather was so cold.

_____   10.   That food is so salty. Should you really to eat food like that?

TEST 62   Problem Words

Clear Grammar 2, Unit 12

Name _____   Date _____

Part 1   Read the short passage. Underline the correct words.

    This (is, are, has, have) a picture of my family. My family is (very, too) large. I (is, are, has, have) three brothers and four sisters. (Almost, Most) all of my siblings are older than I am. I am only older than my little sister, Sara. Of all my brothers and sisters, Sara is my favorite. She (is, are, has, have) only five years old. She is (very, too) tiny, pretty, and smart. Unlike (almost, most) children her age, she rarely cries. When she does, it is usually because she (is, are, has, have) hungry. Her favorite food is ice cream. She would eat it (almost, most) every day if she could.

    I like to spend time with her. We go to the zoo a lot. There we can look at all of the interesting animals and eat all the ice cream we (want, wants). Some people (ask, asks) if it is difficult for me to be a good big sister to Sara. I tell them no. I love my little sister (very, too) much, so it is easy!

Part 2   Multiple Choice. Circle the letter of the correct answer.

1. *Pam:*   Is there _____ much salt in the soup?

    Cassie: No. I think it tastes good.

    (A) too   (C) some

    (B) very   (D) have

2. Jennie went to the doctor _____ some medicine to make her feel better.

    (A) to   (C) for

    (B) have   (D) are

3. The United States _____ a very large population.

    (A) are   (C) have

    (B) is   (D) has

Clear Grammar 2

4. *Alan:* _____ a grocery store nearby?

   Jean: Yes. There is one two blocks from here.

   (A)   There is   (C)   Does there

   (B)   Is there   (D)   Do there

5. I eat healthy food _____ . I rarely eat junk food.

   (A)   most of time   (C)   almost the time

   (B)   most of the time   (D)   some of the time

Part 3   Circle the error in each sentence. Write a correction on the line.

1. Tampa, Orlando, and Miami there are all in the same state.   _____

2. This jacket have two pockets.   _____

3. Bobby is a cold.   _____

4. When we went to the beach, there was a lot of people.   _____

5. She moved to a larger apartment to more space.   _____

Clear Grammar 2

TEST 63   Problem Words

Clear Grammar 2, Unit 12

Name _____   Date _____

1. I listen to the news every night _____ my English.

    (A)   for improving   (C)   to improving

    (B)   for improve   (D)   to improve

2. Because they were driving too fast, they _____ the car in front of them.

    (A)   almost hitting   (C)   most hitting

    (B)   almost hit   (D)   most hit

3. The food in the countries we visited _____ good.

    (A)   was too   (C)   was very

    (B)   were too   (D)   were very

4. _____ a mall in this town?

    (A)   Does   (C)   There are

    (B)   Do there   (D)   Is there

5. She _____, so she went to bed early last night.

    (A)   is tired   (C)   has tired

    (B)   was tired   (D)   had tired

Part 2   Circle the correct form.

1. Susan (had, was) twenty years old before she left Australia.

2. The teacher (is, has) busy now, so he can not meet with you.

3. We are (almost, most) at the top of the mountain!

4. This hamburger is (too, some) big. I can't eat it all by myself.

5. The number of tickets (is, are) limited, so we should buy them soon.

6. (Almost, Most) Japanese eat rice for more than one meal every day.

7. I didn't like the shirt, but I bought it (to, for) give it to a friend.

8. This is a special spoon that is used (to, for) the sauce that goes on top of the peas.

9. My score was 99, so I (almost, most) got a perfect score.

10. The reason for all his school problems (is, are) that he doesn't study very much.

11. (Almost, Most) all of the workers received a 5 percent raise in their salary.

12. I like the food there, but I hate to go to that restaurant because you have to wait (too, very) long to get your food.

TEST 64 Review

Clear Grammar 2, Units 10–12

Name _____   Date _____

Part 1   Write the correct comparative and superlative forms on the lines by each word.

		Comparative	*Superlative*
1.	good	_____	_____
2.	easy	_____	_____
3.	rapid	_____	_____
4.	far	_____	_____
5.	nice	_____	_____
6.	bad	_____	_____
7.	quick	_____	_____
8.	serious	_____	_____

Part 2   Circle the correct word.

1. Since you have to leave early tomorrow, you <u>will / should / would</u> go to bed early.

2. <u>Will / May</u> I use your phone to call my brother? He is waiting for me to pick him up.

3. I have to study tonight, but if I have the time I <u>would / might / should</u> come to the party.

4. It's hot out there! <u>Could / Can / Would</u> you like something cold to drink?

5. When Jan was in high school, she <u>could / would / might</u> play the piano very well.

Part 3   Write *to, for, very, too, almost,* or *most* on the lines as appropriate.

1. Teachers spend _____ of their time helping students and grading papers.

2. Some economists think that Japanese people work _____ hard.

3. This ice cream is _____ tasty.

4. Joan and Kim bought a card _____ their teacher on her birthday.

5. It seems as if I spend _____ all my money at the coffee shop where I study.

6. Recently, plane tickets have been _____ expensive for me to fly home.

7. _____ people like to travel to other countries.

8. Susan used a large wooden spoon _____ stir the fudge.

Part 4 Draw lines between the two parts to make complete sentences.

1. May I use your phone	carry those packages?
2. Can I help you	because I want to stay in shape.
3. I had better not eat dessert	to call my parents?
4. If my car breaks down in the desert,	visit your parents this summer?
5. Will you return to France to	what should I do?
6. If I want to graduate,	I must take a course in auto mechanics.

Part 5 Read each sentence. If the underlined part is correct, write C on the line. If the underlined part is not correct, write X on the line and write a correction above the error.

_____ 1. <u>There have</u> many reasons why people steal.

_____ 2. <u>There are</u> several books on the table.

_____ 3. <u>Do there</u> any reason why there is no class today?

_____ 4. <u>There's</u> many people who would love to go to Hawaii on vacation.

_____ 5. How many pounds <u>have there</u> in a kilogram?

Clear Grammar 2

TEST 65   Review of Book 2

Clear Grammar 2, Units 1–12

Name _____   Date _____

Part 1   Use the time line below to answer the following questions. Write complete sentences.

Carol Barber's Life

1968 born in Tampa, Florida	1975 move to Dallas, Texas	1986 finish high school	1987 move to San Diego, California	1988 buy a dog	1990 marry Tom	1992 first child is born	1992 visit Hawaii on vacation	1994 buy a house	1996 second child is born	Now	2010 visit Europe

1. What is Carol's last name?

    _____

2. How old is Carol?

    _____

3. Why did Carol go to Hawaii?

    _____

4. How many children does Carol have?

    _____

5. What type of pet did Carol buy in 1988?

    _____

6. What is Carol going to do in 2010?

    _____

7. In which city did Carol live the longest?

    _____

100 Clear Grammar Tests **TEST 65**   115

Clear Grammar 2

1. Wendy goes to school every day. She _____ goes to school.

   (A) rarely

   (C) always

   (B) often

   (D) sometimes

2. Can you hand _____ that hammer? I need to put this picture up on the wall.

   (A) I

   (C) my

   (B) me

   (D) mine

3. This knife is dirty. Give me _____ .

   (A) other one

   (C) the others

   (B) the others ones

   (D) another one

4. Bob got a speeding ticket yesterday. He _____ to attend traffic school, or they'll take his license away.

   (A) want

   (C) going

   (B) has

   (D) will

5. You _____ call your mother. She is probably worried about you.

   (A) better

   (C) are going

   (B) should

   (D) ought to

Part 3 Underline the correct answers.

1. Do you know (a, the) price of (Leo's new car, the new car of Leo)?

2. (A, The) best score on (the test of yesterday, yesterday's test) was 97.

3. Due to (the good skills of the players, the players' good skills), our team won (an, the) opening game of the football season last Friday.

4. Perhaps (a, the) word *gumbo,* which refers to a special dish from (Louisiana, the Louisiana), originated in (Africa, the Africa).

5. Because of (the quality of this computer, this computer's quality), it is truly an excellent buy.

TEST 66   Review of Book 2

Clear Grammar 2, Units 1–12

Name _____   Date _____

Part 1   Possessive Forms. Circle the letter of the usual possessive form.

1. A. the car's trunk
    B. the trunk of the car

2. A. the computer's monitor
    B. the monitor of the computer

3. A. Mary's last name
    B. the last name of Mary

4. A. the china's pattern
    B. the pattern of the china

5. A. the gardener's wheelbarrow
    B. the wheelbarrow of the gardener

6. A. tomorrow's news
    B. the news of tomorrow

7. A. Greece's capital
    B. the capital of Greece

8. A. the beach's location
    B. the location of the beach

Part 2   Comparative and Superlative. Underline the correct answers.

1. Texas is (big, bigger, more big, the biggest, most big) than Michigan.

2. Peter is (old, older, the oldest, more older) than Richard.

3. The (intelligent, most intelligent, more intelligent) pet is the dog.

4. Susan and Miriam have (the most, more) fun when they are with each other than
    when they are with their other friends.

5. We live in the mountains of Colorado. Every summer we take a trip to the beaches in
    Florida. My children love to go to the beach. For them, summertime is (happy,
    happier, the happiest) time of the year.

6. I find that Professor Stanley is far (interesting, more interesting) than Professor Smith.

7. That painting is (more lighter, lighter) than the other one.

8. This package is (more bigger, bigger) than yours.

Part 3 Articles. Fill in the blanks with *a, an, —,* or *the.*

1. Tony and Alice are going to move to _____ San Francisco. He has been offered
    _____ new _____ job in _____ electronics. They are very excited to go. Alice
    always wanted to move. She is going to apply for _____ position at _____ junior
    college to teach _____ chemistry. They have a lot of furniture and two cars. They are
    going to take all _____ furniture and _____ two cars with them. They will send
    them by _____ truck, but Tony and Alice will fly.

2. _____ Saturday is _____ first day of _____ weekend in the Western world. In
    some parts of _____ world, _____ Saturday is _____ first day of _____ week. In
    _____ Middle East, for _____ example, _____ week begins on _____ Saturday.
    This means _____ weekend consists of _____ Thursday and _____ Friday.

3. Yesterday was _____ first snowfall of _____ year. _____ avalanche started on one
    of _____ high mountain passes, and many people were cut off by _____ snow.
    _____ air rescue planes had to be called out, and _____ large number of
    paramedics were called in to help with _____ situation. It was amazing that
    no one was killed except _____ old horse.

Part 4 Underline the correct answers.

1. How (far, long) (may, can) you play tennis on a sunny afternoon?

2. (Almost, Most) half of the students in my group bought a present (for, to) the coach.

3. (How come, Why) Shakespeare (write, wrote) that play like that?

4. In my family, we (usually eat, eat usually) (almost, most) of our meals together in the
    dining room. However, sometimes we eat in the living room in front of the TV.

5. (How, What) reasons did he (give, gave) for (miss, missing) (another, other) class
    yesterday?

Review of Book 2

Clear Grammar 2, Units 1–12

Name _____   Date _____

Multiple Choice   Circle the letter of the correct answer.

1. *Joe:*   What did you get your sister for her birthday?

   John: I bought her _____ new mixer because she likes to bake.

   (A)   an   (C)   the

   (B)   a   (D)   one

2. _____ Marcy and June going to go shopping tomorrow?

   (A)   Will   (C)   Are

   (B)   Is   (D)   Do

3. *Mark:*   Why don't we go see *The Fly* at the movie theater tonight?

   Sue: Thanks for the offer, but I _____ that movie last week with Jack.

   (A)   was see   (C)   already see

   (B)   have seen   (D)   saw

4. *Steve:*   _____ did you live in China?

   Ann: Ten years.

   (A)   How many   (C)   How much

   (B)   How long   (D)   How often

5. *Ken:*   Where is Joe?

   Ben: I don't know for sure, but I think he is at the library. Joe _____ studies at the
   library.

   (A)   seldom   (C)   always

   (B)   rarely   (D)   never

6. *Jane:*   Why are you so late picking me up for our date?

   Steve: Well, the professor wanted to talk to Rod and _____ about our final
   project.

   (A)   I   (C)   them

   (B)   me   (D)   Steve

7. Please give me _____ piece of paper. One sheet will not be enough for this test.

(A) other

(C) the others

(B) the another

(D) another

8. _____ is that on the coffee table?

(A) Who's book

(C) Whose book

(B) The book of whom

(D) Whom's book

9. Hotels are expensive in Tokyo, but in London they are even _____ .

(A) expensiver

(C) expensivest

(B) more expensive

(D) most expensive

10. Because I have a test tomorrow, I can't go to the football game. I really _____ study.

(A) may

(C) can

(B) must

(D) could

11. This steak is _____ . I can't eat it all.

(A) too big

(C) very big

(B) very biggest

(D) too bigger

12. *Customer:*   Are all of the clothes on this table on sale?

Clerk: _____ are, but not all of them. You'll have to check the tag on each

                item.

(A) Almost of the clothes

(C) Most clothes

(B) Most of the clothes

(D) Almost clothes

13. You have to be up very early tomorrow for your camping trip. You _____ your

clothes tonight.

(A) will pack

(C) can pack

(B) could pack

(D) had better pack

14. If we had the money, we _____ on a nice vacation this summer.

(A) could go

(C) can go

(B) will go

(D) will be able to go

15. She is _____ and _____ than you. That's why she got into Harvard.

(A) more serious, more smart

(C) seriouser, smarter

(B) more serious, smarter

(D) more serious, more smarter

16. *Abe:*   Whose keys are those?

    Frank: They're _____ .

    (A) my   (C) mine

    (B) mines   (D) my own

17. *Phil:*   The pizza's great. Can I have _____ slice?

    Ron: Well, okay. Just one more slice. Otherwise, there won't be enough for

             everybody.

    (A) the other   (C) another

    (B) other   (D) one

18. Why don't we ask _____ if they need directions? They look lost.

    (A) to them   (C) they

    (B) them   (D) their

19. *Sue:*   Why doesn't Joan ever come to the beach with us on Sundays?

    Mary: Well, she almost _____ plays tennis with Jack on weekends.

    (A) never   (C) rarely

    (B) always   (D) sometimes

20. Last night I _____ home, _____ 20 laps, _____ dinner, and then went to bed.

    (A) drive, swim, ate   (C) drived, swam, eated

    (B) drove, swum, ate   (D) drove, swam, ate

TEST 68   Phrasal Verbs

Clear Grammar 3, Unit 2

Name _____   Date _____

Part 1   Match the phrasal verb on the left with its meaning on the right.

_____ /   1.   Please help <u>put</u> the fire <u>out</u>.   A.   wait

_____   2.   He <u>tore</u> his paper <u>up</u>.   B.   stop trying

_____   3.   You can <u>put</u> the glasses <u>on</u> now.   C.   review

_____   4.   She <u>came across</u> some old pictures.   D.   extinguish

_____   5.   If you need extra help, you can <u>count on</u> me.   E.   wear

_____   6.   She can't <u>put up with</u> her roommate.   F.   find by chance

_____   7.   We should <u>go over</u> the answers again.   G.   depend on

_____   8.   Leslie <u>gave up</u> after the third time.   H.   complete

_____   9.   <u>Hold on</u> while I get my coat.   I.   tolerate

_____   10. I couldn't <u>get through</u> that book.   J.   break into small pieces

Part 2   Add the correct words to complete the paragraph using phrasal verbs.

Yesterday I <u>woke</u> ❶ _____ at 7:30. The first thing I did was <u>try</u> ❷ _____

my new soccer uniform. It fit me just right! Then I <u>put</u> ❸ _____ my lucky

necklace. It was the championship game, so I was <u>counting</u> ❹ _____ the extra

"luck" that my necklace could give me! After that, I went downstairs for breakfast

to make my favorite meal, eggs and toast. I looked in the refrigerator and noticed

that I had <u>run</u> ❺ _____ of eggs. As a result, I ate cereal instead. After breakfast, I

<u>called</u> ❻ _____ my coach, Tom. I had to ask him to <u>pick</u> me ❼ _____ be-

cause my car was broken. I was so surprised when Tom told me the news. The

game was <u>called</u> ❽ _____ because of bad weather! I was so upset with the

news that I went back to bed and stayed there for the rest of the day.

Clear Grammar 3

Part 3   Correct the errors in the following sentences. Write your corrections above the sentences.

1. I look my sister after when my parents are not home.
    after my sister

2. My new hat is in the closet. Put on it to see how it looks.
    it on

3. Hurry! Get on the car before it starts to rain.
    in

4. Billy's piano was beautiful, but he had to give away it because it was too big for his
    it away

    apartment.

5. The students handed on the tests at the end of the class period.
    over

6. The first thing I do when I come home from work is turn it the TV on.

7. When Roger is depressed, he calls his old high school friends on.
    on his old h

8. Luisa ran her boss into at the mall.   *Luisa ran into the mall at her boss*
    into her boss

9. Tony loves baseball, so every time he wants to see the baseball scores he looks it up
    always   *them*

    on the computer.

10. Even though Christopher is my brother, I don't get along him with.
    with him

Clear Grammar 3

TEST 69   Phrasal Verbs

Clear Grammar 3, Unit 2

Name _____   Date _____

Part 1   Underline the correct preposition or verb in the following sentences.

1. *A:* What happened at your interview?

    B: My application was turned (off, down, away).

2. *A:* Do you have your boarding pass with you?

    B: Of course I do. I'd never be able to get (up, on, over) the plane without it.

3. *A:* The weather was bad, so the game was (turned, called, canceled) off.

    B: I hope it will be rescheduled.

4. *A:* Hey, you'll never guess who I just (fell, ran, turned) into at the store!

    B: OK, I give up. Who was it?

    A: Danny Whitfield. Do you remember him? He used to work at the bank.

    B: Of course I remember him. He called me (to, up, on) about two weeks ago.

5. *A:* Don't forget to put (of, on, up) a coat when you go out.

    B: I will (dress, put, make) it on right away.

6. *A:* Will you turn (up, off, on) the television when you go to bed?

    B: Do you want me to (put, turn, make) down the volume? Is it disturbing you?

7. *A:* Why are you working so late?

    B: I am trying to (put, make, add) together this presentation for tomorrow.

8. *A:* Why are you working out so much?

    B: I am going to (make, try, look) out for the team next week.

9. A: Good luck tomorrow! If you don't make the team on your first try, don't give (on, **up**, out), OK?

   B: I won't. I know that some slots on the team might open up later on in the semester because many of the players have to (fall, drop, go) out because they fail their classes.

10. A: Would you set (up, on, with) the tables by the window?

    B: I have already put them (in, away, on). I'll go back and get them.

Part 2   Use the correct phrasal verbs from the box to fill in the blanks.

with	off	out	on	up	at	down

Mary and Tom wanted to take a summer vacation to some place that was special, but they didn't know where to go. They got a sheet of paper and wrote ❶ _____ the names of all the places that they wanted to visit. Before they put a place on the list, both Mary and Tom had to agree on the place. If they didn't agree, they had to cross that place ❷ _____ their list. After an hour of discussion, they came ❸ _____ ❹ _____ a list of ten places. However, this list was too long, so they had to figure ❺ _____ which place was the best for them.

How much is a ticket? How much is the hotel? How much is food? When should they travel? Mary and Tom had to figure ❻ _____ the answers to all of these questions and many others. In the end, they decided ❼ _____ two places: Hawaii and Egypt.

Mary and Tom called ❽ _____ their travel agent. They set ❾ _____ an appointment with her. Last Monday they went to her office. The travel agent used her computer to look ❿ _____ some important information about each place. Mary and Tom looked ⓫ _____ some brochures and listened to the travel agent. They were able to find ⓬ _____ everything that they needed to know in order to make their decision. A month later, Mary and Tom went to Hawaii. They had a wonderful time because they planned their trip so well.

© 2000 University of Michigan *100 Clear Grammar Tests* **TEST 69** 125

Clear Grammar 3

TEST 70   Phrasal Verbs

Clear Grammar 3, Unit 2

Name _____   Date _____

Multiple Choice   Write the letters of all the correct sentences on the line.

_____   1.   A.   Jason turned off the lights.

                       B.   Jason turned the lights off.

                       C.   Jason turned off them.

                       D.   Jason turned them off.

_____   2.   A.   Rene is listening to a CD.

                       B.   Rene is listening a CD to.

                       C.   Rene is listening to it.

                       D.   Rene is listening it to.

_____   3.   A.   Why don't you try these shoes on?

                       B.   Why don't you try them on?

                       C.   Why don't you try on these shoes?

                       D.   Why don't you try on them?

_____   4.   A.   I'm counting Daniel on.

                       B.   I'm counting him on.

                       C.   I'm counting on Daniel.

                       D.   I'm counting on him.

_____   5.   A.   We ran Paula into at the bank.

                       B.   We ran into Paula at the bank.

                       C.   We ran into her at the bank.

                       D.   We ran her into at the bank.

_____   6.   A.   Mario finally got the flu over.

                       B.   Mario finally got over the flu.

                       C.   Mario finally got them over.

                       D.   Mario finally got over.

Clear Grammar 3

_____ 7.   A.   She gave back them.

                       B.   She gave them back.

                       C.   She gave the earrings back.

                       D.   She gave back the earrings.

_____ 8.   A.   Dave tore up the bill.

                       B.   Dave tore the bill up.

                       C.   Dave tore it up.

                       D.   Dave tore up it.

_____ 9.   A.   How did you figure out it?

                       B.   How did you figure it out?

                       C.   How did you figure the answer out?

                       D.   How did you figure out the answer?

_____ 10.   A.   He finally caught up the other students.

                       B.   He finally caught the other students up.

                       C.   He finally caught up with them.

                       D.   He finally caught them up with.

_____ 11.   A.   Who's looking after your children?

                       B.   Who's looking your children after?

                       C.   Who's looking after them?

                       D.   Who's looking them after?

_____ 12.   A.   It took me a long time to catch it on.

                       B.   It took me a long time to catch on.

                       C.   It took me a long time to catch on it.

                       D.   It took me a long time to catch.

_____ 13.   A.   Kids like to make up stories.

                       B.   Kids like to make them up.

                       C.   Kids like to make stories up.

                       D.   Kids like to make up them.

Clear Grammar 3

_____ 14. A. He took off his old shoes and tried on the new ones.

B. He took his old shoes off and tried on the new ones.

C. He took his old shoes off and tried the new ones on.

D. He took off his old shoes and tried the new ones on.

_____ 15. A. When the alarm clock went off, I turned the light on.

B. When the alarm clock went it off, I turned the light on.

C. When the alarm clock went off, I turned on the light.

D. When the alarm clock went it off, I turned on the light.

TEST 71   Past Progressive Tense

Clear Grammar 3, Unit 3

Name _____   Date _____

Part 1   Multiple Choice. Circle the letter of the correct answer.

1. *Jimmy:*   I called you last night, but you didn't answer. Where were you?

    Paul: I _____ my car. It took me over one hour to get it clean.

    (A) wash   (C) was washing

    (B) am washing   (D) was washed

2. *Paula:*   You missed the quiz this morning. What happened?

    Steve: I know. Can you believe it? While you were taking the test, I _____ my tire

               on the highway.

    (A) changing   (C) was changed

    (B) was changing   (D) changed

3. *Barbara:*   Bill, you look really tired! Didn't you sleep last night?

    Bill: There were so many people at my apartment yesterday because my room-

                 mates _____ a party. When I got home from work and saw the fun, I de-

                 cided to join everyone.

    (A) having   (C) was having

    (B) has   (D) were having

4. *Peter:*   _____ you _____ a black motorcycle yesterday? I thought I saw you

                 speeding down Main Street.

    Melissa: As a matter of fact, I was. My car broke down a few days ago, so my brother

                 gave me his motorcycle to use for a few days till my car is fixed.

    (A) Were . . . driving   (C) Did . . . drive

    (B) Was . . . drive   (D) Are . . . driving

5. *Lisa:*   Do you remember what you _____ when the space shuttle exploded in

               1986?

    Mary: I do. I was studying for a test when my mother came into my room and told

               me about the accident.

    (A) were doing   (C) was done

    (B) done   (D) did

Clear Grammar 3

Part 2 Read each sentence and write either the simple past form or the past progressive form of the verb on the line.

(listen) 1. I _____ to the radio when I heard the news about the plane

crash.

2. Last night after dinner I _____ to my new CD.

(play) 3. Little Marcie _____ with her new toys and then went to bed.

4. Little Marcie _____ with her toys when her brother came

into the room and began to fight with her.

(bake) 5. Bo _____ a wonderful chocolate cake!

6. While Bo _____ a cake, I was preparing the main dish.

(drive) 7. _____ you _____ to New York when the storm

started?

8. _____ you _____ to New York by yourself?

(live, neg) 9. Nelson _____ in Mexico a long time. He lived there only a

few months.

10. Nelson _____ in Mexico when the earthquake hit.

TEST 72   Past Progressive Tense

Clear Grammar 3, Unit 3

Name _____   Date _____

Part 1   Write these verbs in the simple past and past progressive tenses.

		Simple Past	Past Progressive
1.	You sing	_____	_____
2.	They drive	_____	_____
3.	I walk	_____	_____
4.	He reads	_____	_____
5.	We listen	_____	_____
6.	She does	_____	_____
7.	It squeaks	_____	_____
8.	You cook	_____	_____
9.	I do not type	_____	_____
10.	He lives	_____	_____

Part 2   Use the simple past or the past progressive tense in the following.

1. I (study) _____ until midnight last night.

2. I (study) _____ when the lights went out.

3. My friends (argue) _____ loudly in the theater when

    someone (tell) _____ them to be quiet.

4. Jonas (eat) _____ an enormous breakfast before going to

    school.

5. We (eat) _____ dinner when the news came on last night.

6. At seven o'clock yesterday evening I (work) _____ .

7. Last New Year's we (travel) _____ in Europe when a family

    illness (end) _____ our trip.

8. The team (practice) _____ for the game last Saturday when

    it (begin) _____ to rain.

Clear Grammar 3

Part 3 Use either the simple past or the past progressive forms of the verbs to complete this paragraph.

Nancy **①** (not learn) _____ to drive until

she **②** (be) _____ twenty years old. She

③ (live) _____ in Atlanta when she

④ (decide) _____ to take her driving test.

She **⑤** (fail) _____ the test the first time

because she **⑥** (hit) _____ another car by

mistake. She finally **⑦** (pass) _____ the test.

She **⑧** (decide) _____ to buy a new car while

she **⑨** (watch) _____ an advertisement on

television. She **⑩** (choose) _____ a big red

truck, but while she **⑪** (go) _____ home, she

⑫ (drive) _____ into the back of a police car.

TEST 73   Review

Clear Grammar 3, Units 2 and 3

Name _____   Date _____

Part 1   Read the meaning of each phrasal verb and then fill in the blank with the missing word.

Phrasal Verb   *Meaning*

1. look   _____   =   be careful

2. run   _____   =   meet by chance

3. get   _____   =   complete

4. put   _____   =   return to the correct place

5. break _____   =   end a relationship

6. put   _____   =   postpone

7. turn   _____   =   increase the volume

8. run   _____ (of)   =   not have any more

9. put   _____   =   return to the original place

10. look   _____   =   try to find information in a dictionary, the

                                         computer, a phone book, etc.

Part 2   Fill in the blanks with the correct words to complete the dialogues.

Dialogue 1

Anna: Please don't <u>throw</u> that scarf (1) _____ . It's one of my favorites.

Bill: Sorry, Anna. I <u>came</u> (2) _____ it while I was looking for my sunglasses. I

        didn't know it was yours. Here, <u>put</u> it (3) _____ . It looks good with

        your outfit.

Dialogue 2

Roberto: Have you <u>checked</u> (4) _____ at your hotel yet?

Lucy: Yes, but it took me almost twenty minutes to <u>fill</u> (5) _____ the regis-

        tration card. It was so complicated!

Clear Grammar 3

Dialogue 3

Marvin: I can't <u>figure</u> (6) _____ this algebra problem, and it's driving me crazy!

Sherry: I'll help you. Ah, here's the problem. You <u>left</u> (7) _____ one of the

variables. You can't solve the problem without that number!

Part 3   Underline the correct words.

1.   While Martha (was driving / drove) to work this morning, she had an accident.

2.   The twins always work together at home. For example, yesterday while Lisa (was

washing / were washing) the dishes, Lucinda (mopped / was mopping) the floor.

3.   While the students (were took / were taking) the test, the teacher (walked / was walk-

ing) around the room.

4.   Michael (was playing / played) a video game when the fire alarm suddenly went off.

5.   What (did she think / was she thinking) when she sold her new car for only two

thousand dollars?

Part 4   Look at the schedule and then write five sentences using the past progressive
tense (one for each of the things on his schedule).

Billy's schedule: yesterday

from 12:00 P.M. to 2:30 P.M.   Study for exam.
from 3:00 P.M. to 5:30 P.M.   Shop for gifts.
from 6:00 P.M. to 6:30 P.M.   Eat dinner.
from 7:00 P.M. to 9:00 P.M.   Do homework.
from 9:00 P.M. to 11:00 P.M.   Watch television.

1.   _____

2.   _____

3.   _____

4.   _____

5.   _____

Clear Grammar 3

TEST 74 Review of Verb Tenses

Clear Grammar 1, **Present, Past, Present Progressive**
Clear Grammar 2, **Be Going to**
Clear Grammar 3, **Past Progressive**

Name _____   Date _____

Part 1   Multiple Choice. Circle the letter of the correct answer.

1. *John:*   What _____ the capital of Romania?

   Sam: I think it's Bucharest.

   (A)   be   (C)   was

   (B)   is   (D)   is there

2. *David:*   How many brothers _____ ?

   Yvette: None. I'm an only child.

   (A)   do you have   (C)   you have

   (B)   have you   (D)   are you

3. *Bobby:*   Tomorrow I _____ to the mall. Do you want to come?

   Gretchen: No, thanks. I'll be out of town.

   (A)   will going   (C)   am going to go

   (B)   going   (D)   go

4. *Brenda:*   Howard, you don't look well.

   Howard: You're right, Brenda. I _____ a cold a few days ago.

   (A)   catched   (C)   am caught

   (B)   catch   (D)   caught

5. *William:*   What _____ last night at 6:00 P.M.? I tried to reach you.

   Keith: Playing tennis. It's what I usually do on Sundays.

   (A)   did you do   (C)   you did

   (B)   were you doing   (D)   were you did

100 Clear Grammar Tests **TEST 74**   135

Part 2 Read the story and then write the correct forms of the verbs.

My summer vacation last year ❶ (be) _____was_____

excellent! I ❷ (travel) _____ with my family to

Europe. We ❸ (land) _____ in London first, and

after visiting England we ❹ (fly) _____ to France.

France ❺ (be) _____ famous for its food, night life,

and museums, so we ❻ (make) _____ sure to visit

everything in Paris. After Paris, we ❼ (go) _____

south to Italy. I will never forget my first day in Rome. While I

❽ (walk) _____ down Via Veneto, I

❾ (run into) _____ Sophia Loren! Her movies

❿ (be) _____ famous all over the world, I think.

She ⓫ (shoot) _____ a film on that street!

I ⓬ (take) _____ her picture and

⓭ (get) _____ her autograph. I

⓮ (regret, neg) _____ going on this vacation

at all! In fact, I ⓯ (look at) _____ my photo

album from this trip all the time.

Part 3 Write complete sentences using the words below. Watch for the tense of the words given to you.

Yesterday / I / go / to the doctor.

1. _____

What / you do / last night at 7:00 P.M.?

2. _____

She / go to work / early / and / come / home / late. (It is her usual routine.)

3. _____

Joe / wash / the car, / paint / the house, / and / study / for exams last week.

4. _____

While / Mary / clean / the house / yesterday, / her roommate / watch television.

5. _____

Clear Grammar 3

TEST 75   Review of Verb Tenses

Clear Grammar 1, **Present, Past, Present Progressive**
Clear Grammar 2, **Be Going to**
Clear Grammar 3, **Past Progressive**

Name _____   Date _____

Underline the correct verb tense.

1. *Quentin:*   Did you hear about the car accident near the bank yesterday?

   Janice: Yes, I did. Laura (calls, is going to call, called, was calling) me last night. I (watch, watched, was watching, am going to watch) TV when she (is going to call, called, was calling, calls) me.

   Quentin: What did she (telling, tells, told, tell) you exactly?

   Janice: She didn't have a lot of news at the time, but she (tell, tells, telling, was telling, told) me what she knew. (Are you wanting, Do you want, Did you want) to go with me to the mall now?

   Quentin: No, thanks. I (am reading, read, was reading, reads) the newspaper now. When I finish, I (am drive, drive, drives, was driving, drove, am going to drive) to my office to get some files that I need.

2. *Darren:*   Are you busy tomorrow?

   Peter: Not really. Why?

   Darren: Some friends and I (going, go, are going to go, went, goes) to the baseball game at Wrigley Field.

   Peter: Let me think. I (am having, have, had) to cut the grass in the morning. What time is the game?

   Darren: Not till 7. It's a night game.

   Peter: I don't usually (doing, does, did, do) anything special, so I want to go for sure! It would be fun to do something different.

3. *Vanessa:* I (called, am calling, am going to call) your house last night, but nobody (is, was, is going to be) there. (Were you going, Did you go, Are you going) out?

    Ellen: Yes, I (am going, go, goes, went) to the mall with Zack and Sam.

    Vanessa: I (try, am trying, was trying) to find you because I (want, wanted, wants) to know if you wanted to go with us to see a movie.

    Ellen: Oh, sorry, but thanks for thinking of me. So did you guys (go, went, going, goes) to a movie?

    Vanessa: Yes, we (see, saw, were seeing, am going to see, sees) *Out of Africa.*

    Ellen: Is that a new movie? What's it about?

    Vanessa: No, it's kind of old, but it's a great movie. It's pretty sad. I mean, the ending is good, but the story is kind of sad.

    Ellen: Did Laura go with you? That sounds like the kind of movie that she (enjoy, enjoys, enjoyed, is enjoying, was enjoying, is going to enjoy).

TEST 76   Review of Verb Tenses

Clear Grammar 1, **Present, Past, Present Progressive**
Clear Grammar 2, **Be Going to**
Clear Grammar 3, **Past Progressive**

Name _____   Date _____

Part 1   Multiple Choice. Circle the letter of the correct answer.

1. I _____ in 1975.

    (A)   am born   (C)   was born

    (B)   had borned   (D)   were born

2. Rob usually _____ a gallon of milk every week. This week he forgot to get some.

    (A)   buy   (C)   does buy

    (B)   buys   (D)   bought

3. You _____ take an umbrella with you. It is going to rain today.

    (A)   ought   (C)   should

    (B)   would   (D)   going to

4. David _____ television when the phone rang. He never got to see the end of the
    show.

    (A)   watched   (C)   watch

    (B)   did watch   (D)   was watching

5. John _____ ready to go to the store for some chicken.

    (A)   is   (C)   has

    (B)   are   (D)   have

6. Mr. Green _____ grammar last semester.

    (A)   taught   (C)   did teach

    (B)   teach   (D)   teached

7. The police _____ you a ticket if you keep speeding.

    (A)   go to give   (C)   are going to give

    (B)   be going to give   (D)   is going to give

8. The telephone _____ . Will someone please answer it?

   (A) ringing   (C) rings

   (B) is ringing   (D) is ring

9. Michael studied very hard after he _____ a bad grade on the last test.

   (A) got   (C) get

   (B) did get   (D) was getting

10. _____ 21 years old to drink alcohol in the United States?

   (A) Do you better be   (C) Do you have to be

   (B) Do you must have   (D) Are you must have

Part 2 Circle the error in each sentence. Write a correction on the line.

1. They were fight when the police arrived.   _____

2. We are going go to the movies tonight.   _____

3. They should to apologize for being rude.   _____

4. The goalie catched the soccer ball.   _____

5. She did talk to her mom last night.   _____

Clear Grammar 3, **Unit 4**

Name _____ Date _____

Part 1 Write the past participle forms in the spaces provided.

Present	*Past*	*Past Participle*
1. begin	began	_____
2. bring	brought	_____
3. buy	bought	_____
4. drink	drank	_____
5. feel	felt	_____
6. know	knew	_____
7. see	saw	_____
8. show	showed	_____
9. speak	spoke	_____
10. write	wrote	_____

Part 2 Read each sentence and write in either the simple past form or the present perfect form of the verb.

(travel)   1. Norma _____ to Pakistan early last year.

2. Norma _____ to Pakistan at least three times.

(eat)   3. I _____ so much over the holidays! I can't wait for them to end.

4. I _____ so much for lunch. I think I'm going to be sick.

(read)   5. Susie _____ all the chapters so far. She's going to do well on the test.

6. Susie _____ all the chapters in one day.

(sell)   7. _____ you _____ your car at the auction?

8. _____ you _____ your car yet?

Clear Grammar 3

(go) 9. Charles isn't here at the office now. He _____

already _____ home.

10. Charles _____ home this morning at 6 A.M.

1. How long (do you live / have you lived) here?

2. Mary (has never seen / never saw) a ballet, but she'd love to one day.

3. (Did the boys come / Have the boys come) to class yesterday?

4. Sheila (has worn / wore) glasses since 1997.

5. In September, Rodney (got / has gotten) married.

Part 4 Use *for* or *since* to complete each sentence.

1. Julia's studied French _____ thirteen years.

2. Robert hasn't seen his best friend _____ 1992.

3. I haven't had a vacation _____ three years.

4. The Smithson kids have owned their dog _____ just over six months.

5. I can't believe you haven't been to the circus _____ you were a child.

Clear Grammar 3

TEST 78   Present Perfect Tense

Clear Grammar 3, Unit 4

Name _____   Date _____

Part 1   Write the correct negative and question forms of the present perfect tense.

		Negative	*Question*
1.	I / sing	_____	_____
2.	he / drive	_____	_____
3.	we / choose	_____	_____
4.	they / fall	_____	_____
5.	you / eat	_____	_____

Part 2   Read the two sentences and then combine them into one sentence using *since* or *for*.

1.   I have a new house. I bought it in 1997.   (since)

_____

2.   Juan studies English. He began to study English three years ago.   (for)

_____

3.   Nina plays the piano. She learned how to play in 1972.   (since)

_____

4.   I love eating sushi. I first ate it in 1993.   (for)

_____

5.   Nancy works at the university. She was hired three years ago.   (since)

_____

Clear Grammar 3

Part 3   A Japanese girl named Midori is traveling in the United States. Her best friend in Japan is named Brenda, a girl from Canada. Brenda speaks English, so of course Midori had to write this letter in English! Read the letter and underline the correct form of each verb.

Dear Brenda,

   Hi. How are you? I'm fine, but I miss you a lot. I am enjoying my visit here in the U.S., and I am learning quite a bit. I ❶ (met, have met) many interesting people since I ❷ (came, have come) here two months ago. My roommate, Lisa, is wonderful. She ❸ (visited, has visited) Japan several times, and she even knows how to speak a little Japanese! Last month, Lisa and I ❹ (went, have gone) to Disney World, and we ❺ (had, have had) a great time. I ❻ (took, have taken) some pictures when we went there, so I will mail them to you as soon as I can. I hope all is well with you. Please write to me as soon as you can.

                                                            Love,

                                                            Midori

Part 4   Read the statement and then write the verb in parentheses in the correct tense. Use simple past or present perfect tense.

(wear)   1.   I _____ this shirt twenty times.

         2.   I _____ this dress on my wedding day.

(catch) 3.   Fred _____ a cold last week.

         4.   Fred _____ the bus every day this week.

(read)   5.   Mike _____ the newspaper this morning at breakfast.

         6.   Mike _____ many Stephen King novels.

(talk)   7.   I _____ to many different doctors about my cat.

         8.   The doctor I _____ to yesterday said my cat is healthy.

TEST 79 Adverbs of Manner and Related Terms

Clear Grammar 3, Unit 5

Name _____   Date _____

Part 1 Rewrite the sentences using a verb and an adverb of manner.

1. Bob has clear speech.   _____

2. They are good dancers.   _____

3. He is a fluent speaker of Greek. _____

4. She is a rapid reader.   _____

5. They are good note takers.   _____

Part 2 Underline the correct adjective or adverb forms.

1. Our school's soccer team plays very (well / good) at home.

2. She talked (nervous / nervously) to her boss.

3. A (loud / loudly) noise woke me up at 3 A.M.

4. Sue is such a good student. She works (hardly / hard) in all her classes.

5. The tourist spoke (slow / slowly) so that the hotel clerk would understand him.

6. Everyone was surprised when Johnny answered the question (correct / correctly).

7. Why did I get a speeding ticket? I was driving my new sports car too (fast / fastly).

8. Every time Bernice gets nervous, she whistles (quiet / quietly) through her teeth.

9. Don't buy that new CD. The musicians in that band play very (badly / bad).

10. Some people say that she is a (good / well) golfer, but I don't agree.

Part 3   Underline the correct words.

1. Mark was able to lose thirty pounds (with diet / by dieting) and exercising.

2. Did you know that you can handle your finances much better (with a computer / by a computer)?

3. (By study / By studying) every day, Sheila passed the entrance exam.

4. We went to New York (by car / with a car), but it took us over twenty-four hours.

5. You can save yourself some time every morning (by not worrying about / by don't worrying about) the clothes you will wear.

6. That restaurant is so popular that you can only get in (by reservation / with a reservation).

7. (By calling / By call) the employment office every day, I was finally able to get a job.

8. Small renovation projects can usually be handled (by small tools / with small tools).

9. One hundred years ago, the only way to travel to and from Europe was (with a boat / by boat).

10. (By not eating / By don't eating) too many appetizers, I enjoyed the rest of the meal.

TEST 80 Adverbs of Manner and Related Terms

Clear Grammar 3, **Unit 5**

Name _____   Date _____

Part 1   Write the adverb forms of these adjectives.

1. beautiful _____
2. good _____
3. extreme _____
4. angry _____
5. bright _____
6. quick _____
7. recent _____

8. stupid _____
9. quiet _____
10. sad _____
11. fast _____
12. new _____
13. slow _____
14. bad _____

Part 2   Underline the correct adjective or adverb forms.

1. The sun shone (bright, brightly) at midday.

2. There was a (loud, loudly) knocking at the door just after the clock struck midnight.

3. Peter had such a (good, well) backhand that he won the game (easy, easily).

4. Maria had (well, great) grades because she worked (hardly, hard).

5. Our neighbors (recent, recently) bought a new house.

6. The principal spoke (angry, angrily) to the students.

7. The (angry, angrily) man shouted at the children after they had thrown stones at his dog.

8. The old woman stared (silent, silently) into space. She was (extreme, extremely) sad.

9. The horse galloped as (fast, fastly) as it could across the fields.

10. James had a bad cold so he felt (bad, badly).

Part 3   Write *by* or *with* on the lines.

1. Did you send the message _____ e-mail or _____ regular mail?

2. Philip plays tennis _____ his left hand and Jay _____ his right.

3. It is better to open the wine _____ a corkscrew.

4. I prefer to travel _____ plane rather than _____ car because it is much quicker.

5. At most places, I can pay _____ credit card.

6. However, at the small gas station near my house, I can only pay _____ a check.

7. The class is going to the Kennedy Space Center _____ bus.

8. Jane won the match _____ her old racket.

Part 4   Underline the correct verb forms.

1. We cleaned up the yard (by cutting, to cut) the grass.

2. The students failed their test (not studying, by not studying) carefully beforehand.

3. The cook created wonderful food (by using, to use) fresh ingredients.

4. I learned to speak Spanish (to spend, by spending) three months in Spain.

5. The writer took four months (by writing, to write) his book about health.

6. Summer is the best time (seeing, to see) the whales in the ocean.

TEST 81   Review

Clear Grammar 3, Units 4 and 5

Name _____   Date _____

Part 1   Read each situation and then write a negative sentence using *yet*.

Situation 1.   Lucy always wakes up at 7:00 A.M. It's 6:45 A.M.

_____

Situation 2.   The boys are taking the test. They still have 20 minutes till the end of class.

_____

Situation 3.   Rhonda wanted to go shopping yesterday, but she didn't have time. She needs to buy some groceries.

_____

Situation 4.   The twins are seniors in high school. They will graduate in June.

_____

Situation 5.   Next month I will travel to Morocco for the first time.

_____

Part 2   Correct the errors in the following sentences. Write corrections above the sentences.

1.   Kendra lives in London for eight years.

2.   That was the worst play I ever see in my life!

3.   Have you ever drove in the snow? It's extremely dangerous.

4.   Although I went to Europe last summer, I didn't travel to Venice yet.

5.   Billy wants to see the new Spielberg film, but I already saw it many times.

Clear Grammar 3

© 2000 University of Michigan   *100 Clear Grammar Tests*   **TEST 81**   149

Part 3   Underline the correct words or phrases.

Jill: How did you do on the test?

Samantha: I have the feeling I did (1) (extremely / extreme) well.

Jill: Really? I bet you studied (2) (hardly / hard).

Samantha: I did. (3) (By use / By using) the extra materials at the library, I got all the information I needed.

Jill: That's great, Sam. You know, maybe I should do the same thing. I didn't do too (4) (well / good) on this test.

Samantha: How is that possible? The teacher even told us that we could take the test (5) (with our notes / by our notes)!

Jill: I know, but I write (6) (terrible / terribly), so I couldn't read my information.

Samantha: I'll teach you how to keep your notes organized and (7) (easy / easily) to read.

Jill: Thanks, Sam. (8) (With your help / By your help), maybe I'll do better on the next test.

Samantha: Well, I'd better go. Let's meet at the library this weekend, and I'll show you how to write more (9) (legible / legibly).

Jill: It's a date. I need to learn this skill (10) (quickly / quick) if I want to pass this class.

Clear Grammar 3

TEST 82 Prepositions after Verbs and Adjectives

Clear Grammar 3, Unit 6

Name _____   Date _____

Part 1   Fill in the blanks with the correct prepositions.

1. *A:* "I didn't know that you wanted me to type the report for you."

    B: "That's what you said the last time. I am fed up _____ your excuses. Do the job correctly next time!"

2. *A:* "We are looking forward _____ visiting you in June. Would you be interested _____ going to a play while we are there?"

    B: "That sounds great. We don't live far _____ a good theater."

3. The president of a university is responsible _____ a variety of things. A good university president should be acquainted _____ all aspects of the American education system.

4. You really need to concentrate _____ your studies. If you continue to ignore your classwork, you will not be happy _____ your grades at the end of the semester.

5. That restaurant is famous _____ its seafood. You can always count _____ them to have the freshest fish and shrimp in the city.

Part 2   Multiple Choice. Circle the letter of the correct answer.

1. *Carol:*   Ugh! I'm not sure I like the way this tastes. I _____ gumbo.

    Henry: Try another bowl. It really is very good.

    (A)   am not used to eat   (C)   am not used to eating

    (B)   not used to eat   (D)   not used to eating

2. I want to thank you for _____ so hard on this project.

    (A)   work   (C)   to work

    (B)   working   (D)   worked

Clear Grammar 3

3. Monica is crazy _____ her new boyfriend. She spends all her time with him.

   (A) with

   (C) at

   (B) in

   (D) about

4. *Tom:* The boss wants to talk _____ you. He says he is disappointed with your behavior.

   Tony: I must be in a lot of trouble. I hope he doesn't fire me!

   (A) for

   (C) about

   (B) to

   (D) of

5. Did you know that drinking a lot of wine can be harmful _____ your health?

   (A) with

   (C) in

   (B) on

   (D) to

Part 3 Circle the error in each sentence. Write a correction on the line.

1. This book full of interesting information. _____

2. Sally is used to live in the United States,

   but now she lives in Canada. _____

3. I am sorry about spill soup on your shirt. _____

4. She is worried to her husband. He's been very sick. _____

5. This shirt is similar for another one I have. _____

Clear Grammar 3

TEST 83 Prepositions after Verbs and Adjectives

Clear Grammar 3, Unit 6

Name _____   Date _____

Part 1   Add the correct prepositions to the verbs below.

1. This book doesn't belong _____ me; it's Lisa's.

2. Have you seen my car keys? I've looked everywhere _____ them.

3. Why do I respect Bob so much? I can depend _____ him whenever I have a

    problem.

4. You're all wet! What happened _____ you?

5. Can you think _____ a good place to eat tonight?

6. Shelley forgot _____ her doctor's appointment, so now she has to reschedule it.

7. The final exam consists _____ one hundred multiple choice questions.

8. If you concentrate _____ the vocabulary, maybe you'll remember it better.

9. I waited _____ my sister all afternoon, but she never showed up.

10. My roommate complains _____ everything!

Part 2   Match the phrases in the right column with the corresponding phrases in the left
column.

_____ 1. Mary is polite   A. in a career in nursing.

_____ 2. I'm so tired   B. about moving to a new city.

_____ 3. She's interested   C. to Davey Jones?

_____ 4. You look familiar. Are you related   D. to everyone.

_____ 5. She's worried   E. of the hot Florida weather.

Clear Grammar 3

Part 3   Fill in the blanks with the correct prepositions.

When I first moved to Canada, I had problems getting used **❶** _____ the
different customs. One day, however, I decided to try to speak **❷** _____ some
of my neighbors. I was surprised **❸** _____ their friendly response. They were
actually happy **❹** _____ meeting their foreign neighbor. In fact, one neighbor
invited me into his home to meet everyone else. I realized that his family was
similar **❺** _____ mine, and that made me feel very good. His children were
very cute and polite **❻** _____ me. His wife brought out some delicious snacks,
and we ate and talked **❼** _____ each other for two hours. This get-together
was so nice that I forgot **❽** _____ my loneliness! I thanked them **❾** _____
their hospitality and invited them to my home the following day. I was very
excited **❿** _____ the new friends I made that day.

TEST 84   Passive Voice

Clear Grammar 3, Unit 7

Name _____   Date _____

Part 1   Answer the following questions. Make complete sentences and use the passive voice.

1.   When were you born?   _____

2.   Where were you born?   _____

3.   What were you called (named)

     when you were a child?   _____

Part 2   Underline the correct verb forms.

1.   The final grammar test (was taken, took) by all of the students.

2.   I have finished all my chores. My bed (is made, made). My room (is cleaned, cleaned).

     My laundry (is done, done). Now I can take a break!

3.   The science class (was finished, finished) the experiment for homework.

4.   The little boy (completed, was completed) the work before his brothers.

5.   Don't worry about the chair. It (was broken, was breaking) before you sat in it.

Part 3   Multiple Choice. Circle the letter of the correct answer.

1.   *Waiter:*   How is your steak?

     Customer: It _____ enough. Can you take it back, please?

     (A)   isn't cooking   (C)   doesn't cook

     (B)   hasn't been cooked   (D)   wasn't cook

2.   Oh no! My wallet _____ . We need to call the police.

     (A)   was stolen   (C)   is stolen

     (B)   stole   (D)   was steal

3.   We were _____ the new movie. You shouldn't go see it. It was too violent!

     (A)   impressing with   (C)   impressed with

     (B)   not impressing with   (D)   not impressed with

Clear Grammar 3

4. They are _____ trying to find a good place to eat.

    (A) tired about   (C) tired of

    (B) tired because   (D) tired to

5. *A:* _____ ?

    B: No, they weren't. What gave you that silly idea?

    (A) Aliens were built the pyramids in Egypt?

    (B) Were the pyramids in Egypt built by aliens?

    (C) The pyramids in Egypt were built by aliens?

    (D) The pyramids in Egypt built by aliens?

Part 4 Circle the error in each sentence. Write a correction on the line.

1. The book was written in 1982 by a writer.   _____

2. I am very boring by this class.   _____

3. We will married on June 22nd.   _____

4. The problem was happened last night.   _____

5. The experiment was do by three famous scientists.   _____

TEST 85 Passive Voice

Clear Grammar 3, Unit 7

Name _____   Date _____

Part 1 Fill in the blanks with the correct passive voice forms.

1. I <u>painted</u> three rooms over the weekend.

    Three rooms _____ over the weekend.

2. Many people <u>signed</u> the Declaration of Independence.

    The Declaration of Independence _____ by many people.

3. We <u>wrote</u> the textbook in 1997.

    The textbook _____ in 1997.

4. They <u>were fixing</u> the radio when the explosion occurred.

    The radio _____ when the explosion occurred.

5. You <u>should take</u> an aspirin for a headache.

    An aspirin _____ for a headache.

Part 2 Underline the correct verb forms.

1. In baseball, the ball (is hit / hits) by the batter before he runs across the bases.

2. Bobby (injured / was injured) in a car accident.

3. The instructor (is teaching / is being taught) the students geometry next week.

4. Your reservations (must make / must be made) at least two weeks in advance.

5. On the TOEFL, the directions (must be followed / must followed) exactly.

6. The burglar (arrested / was arrested) two days after the robbery.

7. For security reasons, all the final exams (are kept / keep) in a safe until test day.

8. Sally (is being driven / is driving) her own car to California.

9. The soccer players (have to be practiced / have to practice) every afternoon after

    school.

10. How many times (have I told / have I been told) you to wear your jacket when it's

    cold outside?

Part 3 Write the passive forms of the verbs in parentheses.

1. This store (close) _____ . Let's go somewhere else.

2. The copies that (make) _____ on this machine are difficult to read.

3. Lisa was married for three years, but now she (divorce) _____ .

4. If eggs (fry) _____ too long, I don't like the taste or the texture.

5. What a beautiful pool! How often (clean) _____ your pool _____ ?

6. Oh no! My wallet (go) _____! Where could it be?

7. Look at Steve sleeping in the back of the classroom. He must (bore) _____ with this lesson.

8. Did you see Lucy at the party? She (look) _____ so happy when she (receive) _____ so many presents.

9. I (tire) _____ last night, so I went directly to bed without studying.

10. When she didn't win first place at the track and field competition, she (disappoint) _____ .

TEST 86   Review

Clear Grammar 3, Units 6 and 7

Name _____   Date _____

Part 1   Add the correct prepositions to the verbs below.

1. The party last night was so much fun. When I looked _____ my watch, I couldn't
    believe it was already midnight!

2. Karen spent over eighty dollars on the opera ticket, but she was disappointed _____
    the performance of the singers.

3. I didn't know you were interested _____ archaeology!

4. I'm sorry I can't talk now. I'm waiting _____ an important phone call.

5. If you're finished _____ your homework, let's go out for pizza.

6. Look, it's Dr. Chancey! She's known _____ her research on bone diseases.

7. I didn't know that Darlene was successful _____ medicine.

8. Bob and Nancy are looking forward _____ their trip to the Seychelles this summer.

9. This book is similar _____ the one I read last month.

10. Gretchen is still complaining about her test score. I'm fed up _____ it!

Part 2   Multiple Choice. Circle the letter of the correct answer.

1. *Ralph:*   Why are you so sleepy today?

    Jane: I _____ my trip to my parents' house.

    (A) am exhausted from   (C) exhausted from

    (B) exhaust from   (D) am exhausted in

2. *Rose:*   Is she single?

    Mark: No, she _____ a millionaire from England.

    (A) married to   (C) is married by

    (B) be married to   (D) is married to

Clear Grammar 3

3. *Omar:*   What's wrong?

   Liz: I _____ the teacher's explanation. Can you help me?

   (A)   am confuse by   (C)   confuse

   (B)   am confused by   (D)   am confused from

4. *Nancy:*   Why did you leave the party early?

   Beth: I _____ the music, so I went home.

   (A)   am bored from   (C)   was bored with

   (B)   was bored from   (D)   bored with

5. *Ned:*   Are you finished _____ the dictionary?

   Stan: Just give me two more minutes.

   (A)   by   (C)   for

   (B)   with   (D)   from

100 Clear Grammar Tests   **TEST 86**   160

Clear Grammar 3, Unit 8

Name _____ Date _____

Part 1 Combine each pair of sentences into one sentence that has a relative clause.

1. The professor just started speaking. The professor is very famous.

   _____

2. The tiger escaped from the zoo. The tiger was finally caught and killed.

   _____

3. This is a great park. We used to visit it all the time in college.

   _____

4. Police officers are honest people. You can go to them when you need help.

   _____

5. He turned in the homework this morning. The homework was late.

   _____

Part 2 Read each sentence. If it is correct, write C in the blank. If it is not correct, write X and write a correction above the sentence.

_____ 1. Where is the girl which you like working with?

_____ 2. Joe was the only person who came to the Halloween party without a

   costume.

_____ 3. The math book which is on the table belongs to my brother.

_____ 4. The suitcase that I wanted to use for my trip it is broken.

_____ 5. Do you know the person from whom he bought his car?

_____ 6. Who's pencil is that?

Part 3 Underline the main (independent) clauses in each sentence.

1. Dali is a painter whose work I really like.

2. I don't know the person to whom this letter is addressed.

3. My friend's pet snake, which was from South America, died last week.

4. I like to wear the blue bathing suit that my brother gave me for my birthday when I

   go to the beach.

5. Who's the person who called you so late last night?

Clear Grammar 3, Unit 8

Name _____   Date _____

Part 1   Underline the relative clauses in the following sentences.

1.   The woman who lives in the apartment above us is very loud.

2.   I want to see the new movie which stars Julia Roberts.

3.   Be careful! The traffic light that is found on that corner is broken.

4.   Have you met the teacher whose grammar book we use?

5.   You can borrow the dictionary that is on the bookshelf.

Part 2   Underline the correct relative pronouns.

1.   *Billy:*   Can you move your car for me, please? It's in a reserved space.

     Sue: No, the car (that / whose / who) is in the parking space isn't mine.

2.   *Lara:*   Where do you want to go tomorrow?

     Zoe: How about going to the new restaurant (whose / who / which / whom) opened last week downtown?

3.   *Marta:* How can you sleep with all that barking?

     Leo: The dog (that / who / whose) barking is so loud doesn't bother me as much as the traffic noise!

4.   *Diana:* Do we need to take notes on the sentences (that / whom / who / whose) are on the blackboard?

     Teacher: Remember, if something is written on the board, it's important!

5.   *Mike:*   Have you tried the new Windart software program yet?

     Lisa: No, the computer (that's / who / whom / which) I use at home is not powerful enough.

Clear Grammar 3

Part 3   Read the sentence and then write a new sentence by including the second one within the first.

1. The architect designed a home. The home is in the gothic style.

    _____

2. Here are the groceries. I bought them.

    _____

3. The dog is friendly. Its tail is wagging.

    _____

4. People don't like snowstorms. They live in the south.

    _____

5. The music was loud. It was played at the party last night.

    _____

Part 4   Put parentheses around the words that are optional in the following sentences.

1. Wendy bought the dress that was hanging in the store window.

2. The plants that are in the garden are dying.

3. The candidate who was elected to office is rather young.

4. People who are working at the university have more vacation time than those who are

    working in business.

5. The girls who were given the prize looked nervous when they got up on stage.

Name _____   Date _____

Read the letter below. Circle the correct form in each underlined pair.

> Dear Dr. Iva Problem,
>
> Six months ago I started **①** <u>dating / date</u> a wonderful
> man, Troy. He is almost perfect. There is just one thing
> wrong with him. He smokes. Normally, I would avoid
> **②** <u>dating / to date</u> a smoker, but when I met Troy, I
> couldn't resist. I enjoy **③** <u>being / to be</u> with him too
> much.
>
> Troy has had a big impact on my life. He has always
> urged me **④** <u>following / to follow</u> my dreams. For example,
> when we first met, I was overweight and had always wanted
> **⑤** <u>being / to be</u> thinner. Troy persuaded me **⑥** <u>beginning /
> to begin</u> **⑦** <u>losing / lose</u> those extra pounds. I did,
> and now I am thinner and healthier than I ever have been.
> In addition, he will do just about anything it takes to
> make me happy. However, the one thing I really want him
> **⑧** <u>doing / to do</u> is to stop **⑨** <u>smoking / to smoke</u>.
>
> Two months ago, he promised **⑩** <u>stopping / to stop</u>.
> I was very excited about his **⑪** <u>quitting / to quit</u>.
> Unfortunately, I was only happy for a short time. Last
> week I caught him smoking. He doesn't know that I have
> found out he is secretly doing this. I really don't feel
> like **⑫** <u>confronting / to confront</u> him about his problem.

Clear Grammar 3

I am tired of ⑬ <u>dealing / to deal</u> with the issue. He
already knows that I don't want him ⑭ <u>smoking / smoke</u> and
that I fear for his health. ⑮ <u>Complaining / To complain</u>
more just won't do anything.

Do you think I should advise him ⑯ <u>seeing / to see</u>
a psychologist? ⑰ <u>Telling / To tell</u> him this would be
very hard for me. However, if you think it is the right
thing to do, I will do it because I love him. I really
need your advice.

Sincerely,

Non-Smoker in Nevada

TEST 90   Infinitives and Gerunds

Clear Grammar 3, Unit 9

Name _____   Date _____

Part 1   Write the correct forms of the verbs in parentheses on the lines.

1.   I didn't know how _____ (do) my math homework, so I called a friend.

2.   They are homesick and often think about _____ (quit) school and

     _____ (go) home.

3.   John wants to learn _____ (play) the violin as well as his brother.

4.   If you want to master English, you cannot avoid _____ (talk) to Americans.

5.   We tried to convince Connie to come with us, but she refused _____ (listen).

Part 2   One of the underlined parts of each sentence contains a mistake. Find it and fix it by writing a correction above the sentence.

1.   I remember <u>to buy</u> a kimono for my sister when I <u>was</u> in Japan.

2.   <u>Talking</u> to friends in different countries <u>are</u> fun.

3.   I suggested <u>going</u> to a movie and even <u>offered paying</u> for him.

4.   <u>Walking</u> is not as enjoyable as <u>to eat</u> is.

5.   Since you seem to enjoy <u>to do</u> my laundry, I have decided <u>to let</u> you do it every week.

Part 3   Indicate whether each verb takes a gerund, an infinitive, or both by writing G, I, or B on the line.

1.   _____ decide   4.   _____ postpone   7.   _____ begin

2.   _____ continue   5.   _____ offer   8.   _____ suggest

3.   _____ pretend   6.   _____ try   9.   _____ intend

Part 4   Put a check mark on the line by the pairs of sentences that have the same meaning.

1.   _____   We have problems, but I will continue to love you.

              We have problems, but I will continue loving you.

2.   _____   Jane had a date, so she stopped studying at the library.

              Jane had a date, so she stopped to study at the library.

3.   _____   John remembered buying milk at the store.

              John remembered to buy milk at the store.

4.   _____   He started to work here in 1997.

              He started working here in 1997.

Clear Grammar 3

TEST 91 Infinitives and Gerunds

Clear Grammar 3, Unit 9

Name _____   Date _____

Part 1   Underline the correct forms.

1.   He promised (to write / writing) me a letter.

2.   Irene postponed (to go / going) on her trip till next year.

3.   To learn gerunds and infinitives, many teachers suggest (to practice / practicing) sample sentences.

4.   Sheila is used to (living / live) in Alaska.

5.   The students hope (passing / to pass) the final exam next week.

6.   Whenever I can, I avoid (driving / to drive) late at night.

7.   We've been thinking about (to transfer / transferring) to another school.

8.   Even though she lives in Florida, Paula enjoys (to ski / skiing).

9.   Luisa decided (to look for / looking for) a new job.

10.   I can't help (to eat / eating) chocolate!

Part 2   Connect the phrases in the right column with the corresponding phrases in the left column.

_____   1.   I avoid   A.   to keep in shape.

_____   2.   I wanted him   B.   eating chocolate cake because it's fattening.

_____   3.   She stopped   C.   take the test again.

_____   4.   Marvin looks forward to   D.   getting married.

_____   5.   The teacher made them   E.   smoking last year.

_____   6.   She goes to the gym   F.   to invite me to have dinner.

Clear Grammar 3

TEST 92 Review

Clear Grammar 3, Units 8 and 9

Name _____   Date _____

Part 1   Underline the relative clause in each sentence.

1.   The police officer who is standing on that corner is my uncle.

2.   Children whose parents will not attend the play can receive a refund for their tickets.

3.   Which book is the one that you wanted to buy?

4.   The cake which is on the table is for my sister's birthday party tonight.

5.   Students who do not do their homework usually do not learn very much.

Part 2   Combine each pair of sentences into one sentence that has a relative clause.

1.   The man is holding the blue umbrella. He is my father.

_____

2.   The book is on the kitchen table. I am reading the book for English class.

_____

3.   The man was holding the winning lottery ticket. He looked very happy.

_____

4.   The dog was chasing the cat down the street. That dog is mine.

_____

5.   I played the violin. My uncle gave me the violin.

_____

Part 3   Read each sentence. If the underlined part is correct, write C on the line. If it is not correct, write X on the line and write a correction above the error.

_____   1.   I <u>expect to work</u> in Japan next year.

_____   2.   We <u>avoid to drink</u> too much soda.

_____   3.   They <u>put off to mow</u> the lawn because it was hot outside.

_____   4.   Cindy and Mike <u>look forward to going</u> skiing in Colorado every year.

_____   5.   The parent <u>refused letting</u> her son stay out past midnight.

Clear Grammar 3

Part 4 Circle the correct form. If both forms are correct, circle both.

1. I remembered <u>buying / to buy</u> it, but I forgot to give it to him.

2. <u>To eat / Eating</u> spaghetti every Sunday is a tradition in her family.

3. They stopped <u>to eat / eating</u> at a restaurant that their friend recommended.

4. Whatever we do, we try <u>to do / doing</u> our best.

5. Drinking a variety of fruit juices <u>are / is</u> good for the health.

6. <u>Say / Tell</u> me how to do this math problem. I'm confused.

7. Kim wants her older brother <u>to take / taking</u> her to the movies.

8. If you decide <u>to work / working</u> hard, you will eventually succeed.

TEST 93 Connectors

Clear Grammar 3, Unit 10

Name _____   Date _____

Part 1   Fill in the blanks with *to, in order to,* or *for.* Sometimes more than one answer is possible.

1. I am studying here _____ improve my English skills.

2. My brother is working _____ save money for school.

3. My sister is reading philosophy books _____ a better understanding of the world.

4. I exchanged my blue shirt _____ a red one.

5. The teacher gives us exams _____ measure our ability.

Part 2   Combine each pair of sentences to make one complete sentence. Use the correct combination of the following connectors: *and . . . too / so / either / neither* or *but.* Remember to use the correct punctuation.

1. Espresso is very strong coffee. Cuban coffee is very strong coffee.

    _____

2. Barbara doesn't have a cold. Warren doesn't have a cold.

    _____

3. Brad has to write a report for class. I have to write a report for class.

    _____

4. They don't need to talk with the teacher. Susan needs to talk to the teacher.

    _____

5. I like to use the Internet to get information for my research papers. I don't like to use the library to get information for my research papers.

    _____

Clear Grammar 3

Part 3 Combine each pair of sentences to make one complete sentence. Use one of the following connectors: *however, therefore, so.* Remember to use the correct punctuation.

1. I studied very hard for my driver's license test. I failed it.

   _____

2. Bob opened the window. The cool air could come inside the room.

   _____

3. You need to pass the next test. You had better study very hard.

   _____

4. Jennifer wanted to take a picture of her friend. Her camera was broken.

   _____

TEST 94   Connectors

Clear Grammar 3, Unit 10

Name _____   Date _____

Part 1   Write *to* or *for* on the lines in order to answer the question *why*.

1. I bought my house _____ get a break on my taxes. It is common for people to invest
    in real estate _____ save money.

2. Suzanne went to the mall _____ a gift for her husband. She went there _____ buy
    a computer game.

3. My brother called me _____ advice on his relationship. He expected _____ get
    helpful suggestions from me.

4. Louise went dancing _____ find some peace and relaxation. For Louise, dancing is
    the best activity _____ peace and relaxation.

5. I usually go to the Japanese restaurant on Milton Street _____ eat sushi. I like to go
    to this restaurant _____ dinner.

Part 2   Write *and* or *but* on the lines.

1. Henry loves working, _____ Freddy prefers to relax.

2. Nancy loves cooking, _____ her sister never cooks.

3. Keith plays tennis, _____ so does Elena.

4. Patti likes chocolate, _____ so does Jean.

5. November is a cold month, _____ so is December.

Part 3 Write the second part of the sentence. Write two answers for each item. Use *too*, *so*, *either*, and *neither* in your answers.

1. I love to play the piano. My sister loves to play the piano.

   I love to play the piano, _____

   I love to play the piano, _____

2. Elephants aren't small. Gorillas aren't small.

   Elephants aren't small, _____

   Elephants aren't small, _____

3. Florida is a hot state. Arizona is a hot state.

   Florida is a hot state, _____

   Florida is a hot state, _____

4. Jennifer doesn't like homework. Elias doesn't like homework.

   Jennifer doesn't like homework, _____

   Jennifer doesn't like homework, _____

5. Brian bought a new house. Nina bought a new house.

   Brian bought a new house, _____

   Brian bought a new house, _____

Part 4 Multiple Choice. Circle the letter of the correct answer.

1. I love watching television. _____ , I have a job that takes most of my time.

   (A) Therefore   (C) However

   (B) So   (D) To

2. I went shopping this weekend _____ I wouldn't have to go during the week.

   (A) therefore   (C) however

   (B) so   (D) to

3. It rained all weekend. _____ , it was impossible for us to paint our house.

   (A) Therefore   (C) However

   (B) So   (D) To

Clear Grammar 3

TEST 95

VERB + D.O./I.O. (direct/indirect objects): *To / For*

Clear Grammar 3, Unit 11

Name _____   Date _____

Part 1   Multiple Choice. Circle the letter of the correct sentence.

1. (A)   The teacher repeated the directions to the class.

   (B)   The teacher repeated the class the directions.

2. (A)   The bank changed me my money.

   (B)   The bank changed my money for me.

3. (A)   The professor asked for Bertha a difficult question.

   (B)   The professor asked Bertha a difficult question.

4. (A)   The bank charged too much in fees this month to me.

   (B)   The bank charged me too much in fees this month.

5. (A)   Larry lent Maria his car while hers was being fixed.

   (B)   Larry lent to Maria his car while hers was being fixed.

Part 2   Find the mistakes in the sentences below and write the corrections on the lines.

1. Shelley opened the door to me because my hands were full.

   _____

2. May I introduce you Joe?

   _____

3. My new electronic dictionary saves for me a lot of time looking up words.

   _____

4. Michelle has written to me many letters this year.

   _____

5. I got for my mother many gifts when I went to Paris.

   _____

Clear Grammar 3

6. Elaine passed the folder for Mr. Klein so he could look at it.

   _____

7. My brother explained me the algebra equation.

   _____

8. Can you do for me a favor?

   _____

9. I can't find my car keys. Please find me them.

   _____

10. Mr. Jones bought to his wife a beautiful ring for her birthday.

   _____

TEST 96 VERB + D.O./I.O.

Clear Grammar 3, Unit 11

Name _____ Date _____

Part 1 Multiple Choice. Circle the letter of the correct sentence.

1. (A) My father bought dishes to me.

   (B) My father bought dishes for me.

2. (A) I tried to explain my sister the answer.

   (B) I tried to explain the answer to my sister.

3. (A) The doctor prescribed the medicine for her.

   (B) The doctor prescribed the medicine to her.

4. (A) I showed the kitten from my nephew.

   (B) I showed the kitten to my nephew.

5. (A) The letter carrier brought me a letter.

   (B) The letter carrier brought for me a letter.

Part 2 Write *to me, for me,* or *me* on the lines.

1. The waiter is getting _____ a menu.

2. Anita introduced her cousin _____ .

3. I asked Ben to do a favor _____ .

4. I didn't understand the question, so the teacher repeated it _____ .

5. He wished _____ luck in my new home.

100 Clear Grammar Tests **TEST 96**

Clear Grammar 3

Part 3 Circle the correct word.

1. Alina (suggested, asked) me to come to her party.

2. Fred (gave, got) a new blanket to Lena.

3. My mother (brought, found) a new shirt for me.

4. Nancy (repeated, pronounced) the word to me.

5. The store (charged, cashed) me too much for my new suit.

Part 4 Read each sentence. If it is correct, write C on the line. If it is not correct, write X on the line and write a correction above the sentence.

_____ 1. Who sold to you your car?

_____ 2. I took my niece to the doctor.

_____ 3. This coupon saved me a lot of money.

_____ 4. When he returned, Fred described his trip to the Caribbean.

_____ 5. Don closed the door to me.

Clear Grammar 3

TEST 97 Review

Clear Grammar 3, Units 10 and 11

Name _____   Date _____

Part 1   Write *to* or *for* on the lines in order to answer the question *why*.

1. Angela went to the United States _____ learn English.

2. Louise went to the doctor _____ medication.

3. Brian went to the party _____ be with his friends.

4. I lent my brother money _____ help him with his bills.

5. Diane called her teacher _____ an explanation of the homework.

Part 2   Multiple Choice. Circle the letter of the correct answer.

1. Fred loves sailing. _____ , he can only sail on the weekends.

    (A) Therefore   (C) However

    (B) So   (D) To

2. Nancy bought a new computer _____ encourage her kids to study.

    (A) therefore   (C) however

    (B) so   (D) to

3. Don studies hard _____ he can do well in school.

    (A) therefore   (C) however

    (B) so   (D) to

4. I want to be healthy. _____ , I eat well and exercise regularly.

    (A) Therefore   (C) However

    (B) So   (D) To

5. Barry works hard, _____ no one was surprised when he bought his new car.

    (A) therefore   (C) however

    (B) so   (D) to

Clear Grammar 3

Part 3 Write *to, for,* or — on the lines.

1. My sister mentioned the party _____ me yesterday.

2. My niece made a birthday card _____ me.

3. As I was leaving, Bernard wished _____ me luck.

4. I couldn't sleep, so my father read a story _____ me.

5. We were relieved when the teacher changed the test date _____ us.

Part 4 Read each sentence. If the underlined part is correct, write C on the line. If it is not correct, write X on the line and write a correction above the error.

_____ 1. I read a book to my nephew until he fell asleep.

_____ 2. Jenny was surprised when the parrot spoke to her.

_____ 3. His daughter's wedding cost to Ted $5,000.

_____ 4. I enjoy doing favors for my friends.

_____ 5. The teacher got angry because my classmate did my homework to me.

Clear Grammar 3

Clear Grammar 3, Units 1–12

Name _____   Date _____

Part 1   Write the correct words on the lines.

1.   It was raining incredibly hard, so the coach called the game _____ .

2.   Kids have great imaginations, so they like to make _____ stories sometimes.

3.   Why don't you try these shoes _____ ? Those don't look very comfortable.

4.   Question number seven is very difficult to figure _____ . Can you understand it?

5.   The cake tasted bad because he left _____ the sugar by mistake.

Part 2   Underline the correct verb forms.

1.   *Sammy:*   Have you ever (flying, flown, fly) on a 747?

     Hector: No, but I (have flown, flew, am flying, was flying) on a 757 when I went to

     Venezuela.

     Sammy: Really? How (was, has been) that?

     Hector: It's a big plane, and it (was, has been, was being) a wonderful trip. Before we

     left, we (were made, made, have made) plans for everything, including the

     hotels and places to visit.

2.   *Sandra:*   Wow, this weather (is, is being) really cold!

     Colin: You're right. I (have never seen, never saw, am never seeing, have never been

     seen) the temperature so low!

     Sandra: Hey, (do you see, have you seen, were you seeing) Kevin today?

     Colin: Yes, I just saw him in the computer room. He (printed, has printed, was

     printing) some letters.

     Sandra: Do you think he (has still been, is still, was still) there now?

     Colin: He might be there, but you'd better hurry if you want to catch him.

Part 3   Of the two underlined parts in each sentence, one is correct and one is wrong. Circle the wrong part and write a correction above it.

1. <u>People who</u> travel <u>with car</u> a lot should maintain the engine.

2. Before a long road trip, it's <u>important for</u> the driver to check the <u>engine careful</u>.

3. <u>By do</u> this before every trip, the driver can reduce <u>unexpected engine</u> problems.

4. <u>To keep</u> an engine running as <u>efficient as</u> possible, it's important to use the proper fuel.

5. When the car is on the road, it's important to watch out for <u>dangerously driving</u> conditions <u>such as</u> heavy traffic or bad weather.

Part 4   Fill in the blanks with the correct prepositions.

1. approve _____
2. belong _____
3. wait _____
4. forget _____
5. complain _____
6. be convinced _____
7. be jealous _____
8. be used _____
9. be full _____
10. be different _____
11. be familiar _____
12. be innocent _____
13. be good _____
14. be sick _____
15. be harmful _____

Part 5   Underline the correct verb forms.

1. I first (heard, was heard) the news about the accident at seven o'clock, but in fact the news (reported, was reported, was reporting) before that.

2. According to the first report, only two cars (involved, were involved, were involving) in the accident, but later reports (stated, were stated) that as many as five cars were in the accident.

3. The report that (broadcast, was broadcast, was broadcasting) at seven o'clock was not very clear because the information was continuing to arrive from the accident scene.

4. The police think that a red BMW (hit, was hit) by a large white truck, but they are not so sure of this.

5. Some think that the BMW (hit, was hit) the truck, not vice versa.

6. According to the most recent police report, the truck (traveled, was traveling, was traveled) east on Highway 603 when the BMW (entered, was entered) the highway.

Part 6 Read each sentence. If the underlined part is correct, write C on the line. If it is not correct, write X on the line and write a correction above the error.

_____ 1. The winter <u>we had</u> last year was milder than this year's winter.

_____ 2. The magazines <u>that he read them</u> contained a lot of new vocabulary.

_____ 3. Many of the people <u>which live</u> near me have exquisite flower gardens.

_____ 4. Players <u>participating</u> in this year's tournament must pay $100 to enter.

_____ 5. Players <u>who are having</u> problems with hotel arrangements should let me know.

_____ 6. Palm trees grow well in <u>areas have</u> a very warm climate.

_____ 7. The name of the <u>director whose</u> company had the most sales is Delores King.

_____ 8. The countries <u>that border</u> on Mexico are the United States, Guatemala, and Belize.

Part 7 Underline the correct forms.

1. *Greg:* Frank, you left the butter on the table. Did you intend (to do, doing, do) that?

   Frank: Yes, I did that on purpose. I wanted (to let, letting, let) the butter (to get, getting, get) a little soft.

   Greg: What for?

   Frank: I'm going to make some biscuits and some cornbread. The biscuits require softened butter, and (so, too) does the cornbread.

   Greg: Well, just be sure to give some of them (for me, to me, me) when they're done!

2. *Anna:* How were your interviews this morning?

   Kevin: The first one went OK, (and, so, but) the second one wasn't too good.

   Anna: What happened in the second one?

   Kevin: It was strange. The man asked (me, to me, for me) a question.

   Anna: That doesn't sound (strange, strangely) to me.

   Kevin: Yes, but immediately after I answered the question, he asked the next one. There was no time in between questions. In fact, it seemed like a race of some kind.

   Anna: Did you try to slow things down (to, by, for) talking about other things?

   Kevin: I tried (to do, do) lots of things, but the interviewer cut me off each time and went to the next question.

   Anna: But the first interview went OK?

   Kevin: I think so. It wasn't outstanding, and it wasn't really bad (neither, either). All in all, I think it went OK.

TEST 99   Review of Book 3

Clear Grammar 3, Units 1–12

Name _____   Date _____

Each sentence contains two underlined parts. Write C above the underlined part if it is correct. If there is an error, write a correction on the line.

1. The car <u>that you bought</u> just last year <u>have had</u> several problems already.

   _____

2. We <u>were enjoyed</u> driving to the lake, and we were able to get there <u>by follow</u> the map.

   _____

3. <u>Have you ever received</u> a <u>gift you</u> didn't like very much?

   _____

4. The accident <u>was happened</u> when I <u>was driving</u> home last night.

   _____

5. I'm <u>accustomed to eat</u> scrambled eggs for breakfast, <u>and</u> my wife isn't.

   _____

6. We <u>were really boring</u>, so we <u>decided to drive</u> to Susan's house to talk to her.

   _____

7. Debbie <u>speaks slow</u>, so it is <u>easily to understand</u> her.

   _____

8. Can you <u>tell me</u> the name of the <u>woman who's husband</u> works at the post office?

   _____

9. I <u>try to avoid returning</u> calls, too, but it's not good to <u>put off them</u> for too long.

   _____

10. <u>For make</u> sure my cold didn't get worse, I asked the doctor to prescribe some

    medicine <u>to</u> me.

    _____

11. I <u>am living</u> here for about two years, and I hope <u>keeping on living</u> here much longer.

_____

12. He's crazy <u>about</u> baseball, so he always tries <u>to attend</u> a local game if there is one.

_____

13. <u>Are you finished with</u> the files <u>whom Dr. Giles</u> gave you?

_____

14. I <u>was embarrassed</u> by what happened, so I <u>left quickly</u> the room.

_____

15. The <u>annoyed</u> sounds that we <u>heard them</u> from midnight till dawn kept us awake.

_____

TEST 100 Review

Clear Grammar 3, Units 1–12

Name _____   Date _____

Multiple Choice   Circle the letter of the correct answer.

1. You have to _____ the fire before it spreads.

   (A) put up   (C) put out

   (B) put off   (D) put over

2. Because there was no food in our refrigerator, we decided to _____ .

   (A) eat in   (C) eat over

   (B) eat at   (D) eat out

3. I'm sorry I didn't get your phone call. I _____ a shower at 7:00 P.M. so I didn't hear it ring.

   (A) were taking   (C) took

   (B) was taking   (D) was taken

4. My family _____ in this house since 1892.

   (A) lived   (C) lives

   (B) is living   (D) has lived

5. I _____ raw fish, but I'd like to try it one day.

   (A) have never eaten   (C) never ate

   (B) am never eaten   (D) has never eaten

6. Cheryl's drawings are incredible! She draws very _____ .

   (A) well   (C) good

   (B) goodly   (D) wellishly

7. Lauren was able to pass the test _____ day and night.

   (A) to study   (C) by study

   (B) study   (D) by studying

8. Spanish was not difficult for Mara because it's not so different _____ her native language, which is Italian.

(A) than
(C) by

(B) from
(D) as

9. One of the biggest differences between Arabic and English is that Arabic _____ from right to left.

(A) writes
(C) written

(B) is wrote
(D) is written

10. Did you know that a Japanese consulate _____ in Miami, Florida?

(A) located
(C) are located

(B) is located
(D) locate

11. I had a very _____ experience yesterday. Let me tell you about it.

(A) embarrass
(C) embarrassing

(B) embarrassingly
(D) embarrassed

12. The little girl _____ in the yard is my niece.

(A) who is playing
(C) which is playing

(B) whose playing
(D) is playing

13. The news report _____ disturbed me.

(A) I saw
(C) seeing

(B) whose I saw
(D) who I saw

14. If we decide _____ for dinner, we'll give you a call.

(A) to going out
(C) going out

(B) to go out
(D) go out

15. After her bad car accident, Susan decided to stop _____ .

(A) driving
(C) to drive

(B) to driving
(D) drive

Clear Grammar 3

16. The teacher made _____ a pop quiz.

   (A) the students to take   (C) to take the students

   (B) take the students   (D) the students take

17. Norman doesn't live here, and _____ .

   (A) neither doesn't Lisa   (C) neither does Lisa

   (B) Lisa doesn't   (D) Lisa does

18. I have so much studying to do. _____ , I can't go out with you tonight.

   (A) therefore   (C) However

   (B) so   (D) Therefore

19. I just moved to a new place! Let me _____ .

   (A) describe to you   (C) describe it to you

   (B) describe it you   (D) describe you

20. I couldn't answer number three on the test. Can you tell _____ ?

   (A) the answer for me   (C) to me the answer

   (B) for me the answer   (D) me the answer

Answer Key

Test 1 p. 1: Part 1. 1. Florida, Arizona, Texas, states
2. Nancy, Jennifer, restaurants 3. book, chair
4. apples, breakfast 5. dog Part 2. 1. are 2. like
3. is 4. eat 5. is Part 3. 1. warm 2. expensive
3. blue, yellow 4. big, red 5. brown, happy Part 4.
1. v 2. n 3. n 4. adj 5. n 6. v

Test 2 p. 2: Part 1. 1. n 2. n 3. v 4. v 5. n 6. v
7. adj 8. n 9. v 10. n 11. v 12. n Part 2. 1. adj, n,
n, adj 2. n, n, n, adj, n 3. v, n, n, n 4. v, adj, n, n, adj
5. n, n, v

Test 3 p. 3: Part 1. 1. are 2. 'm 3. What's 4. am
5. Are 6. isn't 7. it is 8. is 9. 're 10. How's 11. Is
the grammar test 12. is 13. is 14. are 15. is 16. is
17. 'm Part 2. 1. are provinces in 2. is hungry now
3. January has 31 4. of course I am 5. mountains is
the 6. thirsty, but I am 7. they are very 8. the students
are 9. are in North 10. three countries is

Test 4 p. 5: Part 1. 1. is 2. am 3. are 4. is 5. are
6. are 7. am 8. are 9. is 10. are, am Part 2. 1. Yes,
he is. No, he isn't. 2. Yes, we are. No, we aren't.
3. Yes, I am. No, I'm not. (OR Yes, we are. No, we
aren't.) 4. Yes, she is. No, she isn't. 5. Yes, it is. No,
it isn't. Part 3. 1. Are, am not, am 2. Is 3. Are,
aren't, are 4. Are, am, is

Test 5 p. 7: Part 1. 1. catches, wants, try 2. watch,
like, talks 3. go, like, watch 4. trains, practice
5. wash, does, do 6. plays, write, performs Part 2.
1. cook 2. types 3. listen 4. arrives 5. like 6. understand
7. delivers 8. uses 9. jog 10. share

Test 6 p. 8: Part 1. 1. study 2. writes 3. watches
4. think 5. knows Part 2. 1. doesn't 2. doesn't
3. don't 4. don't 5. doesn't Part 3. 1. B 2. D 3. A
4. C 5. B

Test 7 p. 10: Part 1. 1. is 2. are 3. is 4. am 5. are
Part 2. 1. X, Nancy is not a student. 2. C 3. X, This
room is not warm. 4. X, The dog is not black.
5. C Part 3. 1. Are you in class? 2. Are your parents
in America? 3. Is it ten o'clock now? 4. Are you a
student? 5. Am I in your seat? Part 4. 1. Yes, I am.
OR No, I'm not. 2. Yes, they are. OR No, they're
not. 3. Yes, it is. OR No, it isn't. 4. Yes, I am. OR
No, I'm not. 5. Yes, you are. OR No, you aren't.
Part 5. 1. cries 2. watches 3. studies 4. has 5. is
6. does Part 6. Answers will vary. Part 7. 1. Do,
speak; I don't speak 2. Does, study; she does not
study, She studies 3. Does, have; she doesn't have,
She has

Test 8 p. 12: Part 1. 1. Those 2. this 3. those 4. this
5. Those 6. this 7. those 8. This 9. These 10. This
Part 2. 1. that 2. That 3. that 4. that 5. those 6. this

Test 9 p. 14: Part 1. 1. this 2. these 3. this 4. these
5. this 6. these 7. this 8. these Part 2. 1. that
2. those 3. those 4. that 5. that 6. those 7. that
8. those Part 3. 1. This, That 2. This, That 3. These,
Those 4. These, Those 5. This, that 6. This, That
7. These, Those 8. These, Those

Test 10 p. 15: Part 1. 1. my 2. her 3. their 4. his
(OR her OR its) 5. your 6. our 7. their 8. Her
9. their 10. our 11. their 12. her 13. our 14. their
15. their Part 2. 1. My 2. their 3. Our 4. His
5. Our 6. Your 7. My 8. Her, Her 9. Your
10. Their

Test 11 p. 17: Part 1. 1. C 2. X; Jessica's shirt is
pretty. 3. X; Her name is Angela. 4. X; Our house
is in Tampa. 5. C Part 2. 1. her 2. my 3. Their
4. They 5. I Part 3. 1. Her 2. My 3. Their 4. Our
5. his

Test 12 p. 18: Part 1. 1. These 2. That 3. Those
4. This 5. These 6. Those 7. That 8. this 9. These
10. that Part 2. 1. your 2. my 3. our 4. Their
5. her 6. his Part 3. 1. X; He understands it. 2. X;
We ate it all. 3. C 4. C 5. X; Your bicycle is very
good. 6. C 7. X; These books are too heavy for
me to carry. 8. C 9. X; That chicken lays eggs
every morning. 10. X; These earrings are too
heavy for my ears.

Test 13 p. 20: Part 1. 1. was 2. was 3. was 4. was
5. were 6. were Part 2. 1. is = was 2. were = was
3. don't was = was not 4. were = was 5. don't
were = was not Part 3. 1. was not 2. were not
3. were not 4. was not 5. was not Part 4. 1. Was it
hot yesterday? Yes, it was. / No, it wasn't. 2. Were
you late for class yesterday? Yes, I was. / No, I
wasn't. 3. Was the teacher happy yesterday? Yes, she
was. / No, she wasn't. 4. Was the news interesting
yesterday? Yes, it was. / No, it wasn't. 5. Was the sky
blue yesterday? Yes, it was. / No, it wasn't.

Test 14 p. 22: Part 1. 1. was 2. are 3. was 4. is
5. were 6. am 7. were 8. is Part 2. 1. weren't
2. wasn't 3. weren't 4. wasn't 5. wasn't 6. weren't
Part 3. 1. Was the restaurant open yesterday?
2. Were they busy yesterday? 3. Were the lions
very sleepy yesterday? 4. Was the dog very hungry
yesterday? 5. Were Tim and Mike very happy
yesterday?

Test 15 p. 23: Part 1. 1. read 2. do 3. spent 4. spoke
5. left 6. sold 7. chose 8. bought Part 2. 1. studied,
wrote, talked, told, went, got, slept 2. went, was,
met (OR saw), came, saw, come (OR came),
believe, brought, called

189

Test 16 p. 24: Part 1. 1. walked 2. baked 3. helped 4. finished 5. proved 6. needed 7. entered 8. shaved 9. talked 10. smiled 11. listened 12. phoned 13. cooked 14. waited 15. repeated 16. asked Part 2. 1. came 2. flew 3. visited 4. roamed 5. tried 6. talked 7. dropped 8. saw Part 3. 1. brought 2. caught 3. chose 4. knew 5. ate 6. laid 7. thought 8. got 9. flew 10. had 11. grew 12. shook 13. paid 14. rode 15. heard 16. hid 17. forgot 18. ran 19. sold 20. slept

Test 17 p. 26: Part 1. 1. went, was, took, were, spent, were, drank, bought 2. had, came, wore, was, sat, said, said, looked, put, took, gave, was, saw, was Part 2. 1. I didn't 2. they weren't 3. he wasn't 4. they didn't 5. I didn't

Test 18 p. 28: Part 1. 1. France and England are two countries in Europe. 2. I am not hungry because I ate dinner at 5.00. 3. My favorite color for pants is black. 4. Are you hungry? 5. Are you in America? Part 2. 1. X; Do your parents speak English? 2. X; Does your brother like to dance? 3. C 4. X; Do you want to travel? No, I do not. 5. X; My mother doesn't play the piano. Part 3. 1. this 2. Those 3. These 4. That 5. This Part 4. 1. My 2. Our 3. He 4. Her 5. They Part 5. 1. X; Today it is hot, but yesterday it was not very hot. 2. C 3. X; I was not happy before I learned how to use the computer. 4. X; Were you sad yesterday? 5. C Part 6. 1. studied 2. watched 3. played 4. stopped 5. danced 6. needed 7. tried 8. hopped 9. hoped 10. wished Part 7. 1. Did you like to dance when you were in junior high school? No, I didn't. 2. Did your mother cook for you when you were young? No, she didn't. 3. Did your parents call you last night? No, they didn't. 4. Did your mother and father speak English at home when you were young? No, they didn't. 5. Did your grandparents visit America before you were born? No, they didn't.

Test 19 p. 30: Part 1. C, received, failed, wrote, C, C, C, didn't feel, had, C, didn't help, C, wants Part 2. my, that, my, this, my, her, her, that, That, these, my, your

Test 20 p. 32: Part 1. 1. What 2. Where 3. which 4. Why 5. What Part 2. 1. What does huge mean? 2. Where did you work last year? 3. Where were you born? 4. When is the grammar exam? 5. Why did Samantha do that? Part 3. 1. What is her new phone number? 2. What is her job? OR What is her occupation? OR What does she do? 3. Where does she work? 4. When was she born? 5. Who was her favorite professor in medical school?

Test 21 p. 34: Part 1. 1. Where 2. When 3. Who 4. Why 5. What Part 2. 1. What is Valerie's major? 2. Where is the dog? 3. When (OR What time) do you (OR I) go to sleep? 4. Who is your (OR my) favorite teacher? 5. Why does Nina eat chocolate? Part 3. 1. B 2. C 3. A 4. D 5. B

Test 22 p. 36: Part 1. 1. We eat dinner in the kitchen at 6:00 P.M. 2. I study at the University of South Florida in Tampa. 3. My sister lives in an apartment on Fowler Ave. 4. My appointment is at 11:00 in the morning. 5. The apples were in the refrigerator yesterday. Part 2. 1. We lived in a small house on Fletcher Ave. in 1970. 2. My brother bought a big boat last year. 3. Nora baked a delicious cake in her new kitchen last night. 4. My mother has a large garden. 5. My sister has a blue house. Part 3. 1. X; large house 2. X; delicious cookies 3. C 4. X; here at noon 5. C 6. X; large university 7. X; am hungry 8. C 9. C 10. X; These shoes are expensive. OR These are expensive shoes.

Test 23 p. 38: Part 1. 1. She has class at the university at 5 P.M. 2. He has lunch here after class. 3. The book is on the table in the room. 4. They live in a house on 50th Street. 5. I drink coffee in my office in the morning. 6. Ms. Robinson likes to sit in first class on a 747. 7. They use software in the computer lab every day. 8. She lives in a small house. 9. We often eat dinner at the same table in the Indian restaurant on Main Street. 10. He practices typing from 4 to 5 every day. Part 2. 1. On Siena Street she lives. = She lives on Siena Street. 2. a large house blue = a large blue house 3. in the morning to read a newspaper = to read a newspaper in the morning

Test 24 p. 39: Part 1. 1. Who 2. Where 3. Why 4. What 5. When Part 2. 1. C 2. X; Where do you go to sleep at night? 3. X; What does *fib* mean? 4. C 5. X; What does Suzanne have in the box? Part 3. 1. I live in a small apartment. 2. I was born at 10 A.M. on July 18th. 3. Maria studies psychology in the library every night. 4. The students go to class every day. 5. Fred bought a beautiful dog. Part 4. 1. C 2. X; These are beautiful glasses. 3. C 4. Margo has two small dogs. 5. David teaches in this school every day.

Test 25 p. 41: Part 1. 1. are standing 2. are saying 3. X 4. is listening 5. X 6. X 7. am repeating 8. are taking 9. X 10. X Part 2. 1. is eating 2. eats 3. write 4. am writing 5. believe 6. believe 7. uses 8. is using 9. need 10. need

Test 26 p. 42: Part 1. 1. is studying 2. studies 3. drinks 4. is drinking 5. eats 6. is eating 7. is listening 8. listens 9. is playing 10. plays Part 2. 1. Are Yoko and Ichiko speaking English with each other? Yes, they are. 2. Is it raining now? No, it isn't. 3. Do you love your mother? Yes, I do. 4. Do you need food and water? Yes, I do. 5. Is Steve watching television? No, Steve isn't. Part 3. 1. C 2. X; The cats are not eating their food right now. 3. X; I need a new car. 4. X; Is Sheila going to the store now? 5. C Part 4. 1. opening 2. sitting 3. X 4. eating 5. dancing 6. watching 7. X 8. helping 9. X 10. X

Test 27 p. 44: Part 1. 1. some 2. an, a few 3. much 4. any 5. a lot of Part 2. 1. D 2. A 3. C 4. C 5. D Part 3. 1. much = a lot of 2. is = are 3. has very = has a very 4. are a books = are books 5. some = any

Test 28 p. 46: Part 1. 1. a 2. some 3. an 4. some 5. an 6. some 7. a Part 2. 1. many 2. much 3. much 4. much 5. many 6. many 7. much Part 3. 1. a few 2. a few 3. a little 4. a little 5. a little 6. a few 7. a few

Test 29 p. 47: Part 1. 1. on 2. in 3. in 4. on 5. at

6. in 7. at 8. in 9. on 10. at OR in Part 2. Answers will vary. 1. I was born on January 29. 2. I live in Tampa. 3. I get up at 6 A.M. every day. 4. I study English at the English Language Institute. 5. My school is located on Huron Avenue. Part 3. 1. on, I live at 1307 Clifford Avenue. 2. at, Call me in the morning. 3. at, Bob lives in Paris. 4. in the, I don't like to go out at night. 5. in, We need to meet them at 5:00.

Test 30 p. 49: Part 1. 1. at 2. at 3. in 4. in 5. at 6. on 7. on 8. in 9. at 10. in Part 2. 1. on 2. on 3. on, in 4. in 5. in 6. at 7. at 8. on 9. at, on 10. on

Test 31 p. 50: Part 1. 1. study 2. am studying 3. has 4. has 5. explains 6. is explaining 7. want 8. want Part 2. 1. much 2. a lot of 3. a little 4. a little 5. many 6. a lot of 7. a little 8. many Part 3. 1. in 2. at 3. on 4. on 5. in 6. on 7. at 8. at 9. at 10. in 11. in 12. in

Test 32 p. 52: Part 1. 1. D 2. B 3. A 4. C 5. B Part 2. 1. this 2. That 3. These 4. those 5. this Part 3. 1. your 2. Their 3. I 4. Our 5. He Part 4. 1. X; no was = wasn't 2. X; was walk = walked 3. C 4. X; cryed = cried 5. X; don't was = wasn't Part 5. 1. Where is your little sister? 2. Why are you studying English? 3. Who is your favorite actor? 4. When is your birthday? 5. What does *startle* mean? Part 6. 1. Are Juan and Manuel speaking English now? Yes, they are. 2. Does your mother like asparagus? No, she doesn't. 3. Does Ann want a gift? Yes, she does. 4. Is it snowing now? No, it isn't. 5. Is Ryan playing football? Yes, he is. Part 7. 1. X; a little homework 2. X; many books 3. C 4. C 5. X; a beautiful new car Part 8. 1. in 2. at, in 3. in 4. on, in 5. at, on

Test 33 p. 55: 1. flowers = flower 2. doesn't = isn't 3. she = her 4. weared = wore 5. Do = Does 6. Does = Is 7. these = this 8. Is = Does 9. is = are 10. book = books 11. any = some 12. those = that 13. were = was 14. they're = their 15. much = many 16. I = my 17. fail = failed 18. are = were 19. What = Where 20. countries a = countries is a 21. understood = understand 22. am not knowing = don't know 23. an examination difficult = a difficult examination 24. on = in 25. in the night = at night 26. very much that kind of music = that kind of music very much 27. do = are 28. had wonderful = had a wonderful 29. don't had = didn't have 30. Did = Were 31. you learned = did you learn 32. no is = is not 33. flight number 882 arrived = did flight number 882 arrive 34. dessert favorite = favorite dessert 35. help = am helping 36. in = on

Test 34 p. 57: 1. B 2. B 3. B 4. B 5. C 6. A 7. D 8. C 9. D 10. A 11. B 12. C 13. B 14. A 15. D 16. D 17. C 18. A 19. A 20. B

Test 35 p. 60: Part 1. 1. The, the, — 2. the, the 3. an, a 4. the, a 5. a 6. a, the, — 7. the, the 8. —, the 9. the, — 10. the, — Part 2. 1. a 2. a 3. an 4. a 5. a 6. a 7. an 8. a 9. a 10. a 11. a 12. an

Test 36 p. 61: Part 1. 1. the, the, —, the 2. a, a, —, the, —, — 3. —, —, —, —, an, a 4. —, —, —

5. the, the, a , — , an, a Part 2. 1. The month of January has 31 days. 2. The white Bengal tiger cub is a cute animal. 3. Skiing is fun to do in winter (OR the winter). 4. I prefer to go to the beach in summer (OR the summer). 5. My favorite food is pasta with tomato and meat sauce. 6. Thanksgiving is a holiday when many Americans eat a big meal. 7. Canada is in North America and so is Mexico. 8. Costa Rica and Belize are in Central America. 9. One of the main languages that people speak in Algeria is Berber. 10. Jogging is one of the most popular forms of exercise. Part 3. 1. X; a sandwich 2. X; India 3. C 4. X; The beach 5. C 6. C

Test 37 p. 63: Part 1. 1. B 2. C 3. A 4. D 5. B Part 2. 1. I am going to study tonight. (Answers may vary.) 2. Yes, I am going to go out this weekend. (No, I am not going to go out this weekend.) 3. I am going to take a vacation. 4. No, my family is not going to visit here. OR Yes, my family is going to visit here. 5. The class is going to study the next chapter in the grammar book next Monday. Part 3. 1. get = to get 2. going to go = went 3. Do = Are 4. are = is 5. you are = are you

Test 38 p. 65: Part 1. 1. every day 2. tonight 3. last month 4. tonight 5. last year 6. right now 7. goes 8. am eating 9. visit 10. played 11. is going to be 12. have Part 2. 1. X; Shirts are going to be on sale tomorrow (OR today). (OR Shirts were on sale yesterday.) 2. X; Are Joe and Sarah going to go out tonight? 3. X; What are we going to do after dinner? 4. C Part 3. 1. Are they going to go to a concert together? 2. Is Jane going to attend her class reunion? 3. Are we going to do our homework together? 4. Are you going to listen to your favorite CD tonight? 5. Is Larry going to study for a big exam after dinner?

Test 39 p. 67: Part 1. 1. —, —, the, the 2. a, the 3. The, the, — 4. The, the 5. the, — Part 2. 1. an 2. — 3. a 4. — 5. a 6. — 7. a 8. a 9. a Part 3. 1. X; is going 2. C 3. X; are not going 4. C 5. X; are going Part 4. 1. is snowing 2. visited 3. are going to eat 4. speak 5. are going to play

Test 40 p. 69: Part 1. 1. spoke 2. lost 3. sent 4. fly 5. heard Part 2. 1. get 2. got 3. eat 4. had 5. left 6. drove 7. heard 8. stopped 9. knew 10. was 11. called 12. came 13. were 14. repaired 15. cost 16. arrived 17. was 18. explained 19. didn't get 20. is 21. like Part 3. 1. Mary gave him a card 2. Rick didn't know her last name 3. I went to the store 4. she didn't find her book bag 5. they broke the window 6. he didn't become sick 7. the shirt cost a lot 8. I didn't take the bus to work

Test 41 p. 71: Part 1. 1. knew 2. found 3. read 4. ate 5. drank 6. met 7. sang 8. flew 9. slept 10. lost 11. came 12. won Part 2. 1. rode 2. stood 3. rang 4. made 5. shot 6. spent 7. tore 8. understood Part 3. 1. flew 2. took 3. was 4. was 5. stayed 6. came 7. spoke 8. was 9. were 10. ate 11. were 12. took 13. saw 14. climbed 15. was 16. loved (OR love) 17. want

Test 42 p. 73: Part 1. 1. assisted 2. are going to 3. cut 4. ate 5. were 6. drives 7. loves 8. were

9. cried 10. is making Part 2. 1. go 2. costs 3. have
4. went 5. cost 6. paid 7. were 8. enjoy 9. are
coming to 10. left 11. am going to see

Test 43 p. 75: Part 1. 1. C 2. A 3. D 4. D 5. B
Part 2. 1. received 2. am taking 3. have 4. is 5. are
6. are coming 7. are studying 8. closes 9. have
10. Do, remember 11. had 12. stayed 13. did not
go (OR didn't go) 14. told 15. is going to come
16. do not have (OR don't have) 17. wanted

Test 44 p. 77: Part 1. 1. are you 2. I am doing 3. I
have 4. do you want 5. are you going to do 6. I
don't know. 7. I went 8. We decided 9. Do you
want 10. Do many people 11. I'm not 12. you
and Nedra had 13. It was 14. were there 15. We
had 16. we want 17. It sounds 18. I'm going to
go (OR I'll go) Part 2. 1. C 2. X; didn't have 3. C
4. X; wrapped 5. X; wakes

Test 45 p. 79: Part 1. 1. much 2. tall 3. often 4. far
5. old Part 2. 1. How far did Michael and Kim jog?
2. How long did it take to build the Taj Mahal?
3. How tall is Mount Everest? 4. How much sugar
does Mom need to make Lisa's birthday cake?
5. How often does the chess club meet? Part 3.
1. you go = do you go 2. What = How 3. long =
far 4. much = many 5. high = tall

Test 46 p. 81: Part 1. 1. much 2. long 3. tall 4. far
5. many 6. much 7. old 8. often 9. big 10. long
Part 2. 1. How old is the puppy? 2. How much
does Kent weigh? 3. How often did Lin study
English in high school? 4. How tall is Matt?
5. How far is it to the next town? 6. How many
pounds are there in a kilo? 7. How many tests are
there in this textbook? 8. How long did they date
before they got married? 9. How crowded was the
mall before the holidays? 10. How fast (OR How
many miles per hour) do you usually drive?

Test 47 p. 83: Part 1. 1. became 2. brought 3. meant
4. ran 5. came 6. read 7. threw 8. told 9. shut
10. put 11. saw 12. made 13. built 14. blew
15. bought 16. chose 17. wore 18. won 19. spread
20. flew Part 2. 1. went 2. saw 3. was 4. was
5. felt 6. closed 7. fell 8. slept 9. moved 10. had
11. swam Part 3. 1. deep 2. much 3. far 4. old
5. often 6. far 7. many 8. much

Test 48 p. 85: Part 1. 1. D 2. F 3. B 4. C 5. E 6. A
Part 2. 1. The students always study in the library.
2. I am always happy. 3. The teacher is rarely in her
office after class. 4. You will usually find Jun at his
favorite coffee shop. Part 3. 1. The students always
do their homework on time. 2. How often do you
study? 3. What time do you usually go to the
store? 4. The grammar teacher always has a book
or paper in her hand.

Test 49 p. 86: Part 1. 1. My dog always likes to eat.
2. On the weekends, we usually go to the movies.
3. Rob and Peter rarely (OR seldom) go to bed
before midnight. 4. I don't often eat breakfast. I
usually have just a cup of coffee. 5. My neighbors
rarely use their swimming pool. It is usually empty.
6. On Sunday mornings, I usually wash my car.
7. Mary and Louise never do their English homework! Part 2. 1. never 2. always 3. sometimes

4. usually 5. rarely (OR seldom) 6. often 7. seldom (OR rarely) Part 3. 1. usually take 2. always
read 3. usually occur 4. never go 5. seldom gives
6. rarely fail 7. sometimes practice 8. are often
9. usually rollerblade 10. can never

Test 50 p. 88: Part 1. 1. her 2. Our 3. my 4. He
5. My, me 6. him 7. They 8. We, it Part 2. 1. We,
it 2. She, her 3. our 4. his, He 5. her 6. They, it
Part 3. 1. her = she 2. we = us 3. I = me 4. he =
him 5. Me = I

Test 51 p. 89: Part 1. 1. D 2. F 3. A 4. G 5. B 6. E
7. C Part 2. 1. them 2. her 3. us, them 4. her
5. me 6. it 7. them 8. them 9. him 10. me, her
Part 3. 1. C 2. X; us 3. X; him 4. C 5. X; them
6. C 7. C 8. X; him

Test 52 p. 91: Part 1. 1. always play 2. rarely drink
3. is always 4. rarely rains 5. never eat 6. sometimes eat 7. always makes 8. always rains 9. usually
(OR always) gets Part 2. 1. us 2. My 3. He 4. you
5. They 6. She 7. It 8. My Part 3. me family = my
family, her friend = his friend, us sail boat = their
sailboat, in him = in it, My wife and me = My
wife and I, us chairs = our chairs, It was good =
They were good, Her was alone = She was alone,
her was bored = she was bored.

Test 53 p. 93: Part 1. 1. B 2. C 3. C 4. A 5. C
Part 2. 1. another 2. Others 3. the other 4. one
5. it 6. The others (OR Others) 7. Others 8. another (OR the other) 9. it 10. another Part 3.
1. one = it 2. other = another 3. one = it
4. another = the other 5. other = another

Test 54 p. 95: Part 1. 1. another 2. one 3. It 4. it
5. one 6. the other Part 2. 1. X; the other one
2. X; Other 3. C 4. X; other 5. X; another Part 3.
1. another 2. it, other 3. one (OR other) 4. the
other 5. others

Test 55 p. 97: Part 1. 1. B 2. C 3. A 4. B 5. C
Part 2. 1. Michael's dog is black and white. 2. Mr.
Erb's house is very big. 3. Laura's hobby is stamp
collecting. 4. Rachel's mail is from Japan. (OR
The mail from Japan is Rachel's.) 5. The bird's nest
is high in the oak tree. Part 3. The magazine's
price = The price of the magazine, only magazine
of Adventure Publishers = Adventure Publishers'
only magazine, That magazine's name = The name
of that magazine

Test 56 p. 99: Part 1. 1. I 2. He 3. You 4. They
5. We 6. She Part 2. 1. my 2. his 3. my 4. her
5. my 6. their Part 3. 1. end of the movie
2. whose 3. basketball player's car 4. their, mine
5. your, Mine, sister's, hers 6. Whose 7. hers

Test 57 p. 100: Part 1. 1. it 2. other 3. one
4. another 5. another 6. other Part 2. 1. whose
2. mine, hers 3. their Part 3. 1. X; price of the car
2. X; top of the table 3. C 4. C 5. X; mine 6. C
7. X; the name of the hotel 8. X; dog's

Test 58 p. 102: Part 1. 1. darker than 2. the darkest
3. smaller than 4. the biggest 5. the shortest
6. longer than 7. fewer 8. less popular than 9. the
most popular Part 2. 1. slower than 2. the fastest
3. the worst 4. farther than 5. farthest 6. the
fewest 7. less than 8. the least 9. the best

Test 59 p. 104: Part 1. 1. taller 2. the most interesting 3. better 4. more intelligent 5. faster Part 2. 1. X; This is an easier way of solving that math problem. 2. C 3. X; Mr. Jones is the nicest teacher in the school. 4. X; Parents are usually wiser than their children. 5. X; I like this chair best because it is the most comfortable. Part 3. 1. more delicious, the most delicious 2. worse, the worst 3. more tired, the most tired 4. more pleasant, the most pleasant 5. farther, the farthest Part 4. 1. smaller 2. more expensive 3. the biggest (other answers are possible, but all should be in the superlative form)

Test 60 p. 106: Part 1. 1. C 2. B 3. D 4. D 5. C 6. D 7. C 8. B 9. B 10. D Part 2. 1. can't 2. will 3. would 4. shouldn't 5. Would 6. might 7. may 8. am going 9. would 10. had better

Test 61 p. 108: Part 1. 1. should 2. must 3. might 4. will 5. had better Part 2. 1. May I 2. can we 3. should they 4. can Ann Part 3. 1. C 2. X; leave 3. X; they have to study for a test 4. C 5. C 6. X; might not go 7. X; ought to use 8. C 9. X; we had to buy 10. X; Should you really eat

Test 62 p. 109: Part 1. is, very, have, Almost, is, very, most, is, almost, want, ask, very Part 2. 1. A 2. C 3. D 4. B 5. B Part 3. 1. there are all = are all 2. have two pockets = has two pockets 3. is a cold = has a cold (OR is cold) 4. there was = there were 5. to more space = for more space (OR to have more space)

Test 63 p. 111: Part 1. 1. D 2. B 3. C 4. D 5. B Part 2. 1. was 2. is 3. almost 4. too 5. is 6. Most 7. to 8. for 9. almost 10. is 11. Almost 12. too

Test 64 p. 113: Part 1. 1. better, the best 2. easier, the easiest 3. more rapid, the most rapid 4. farther, the farthest 5. nicer, the nicest 6. worse, the worst 7. quicker, the quickest 8. more serious, the most serious Part 2. 1. should 2. May 3. might 4. Would 5. could Part 3. 1. most 2. too 3. very 4. for 5. almost 6. too 7. Most 8. to Part 4. 1. May I use your phone to call my parents? 2. Can I help you carry those packages? 3. I had better not eat dessert because I want to stay in shape. 4. If my car breaks down in the desert, what should I do? 5. Will you return to France to visit your parents this summer? 6. If I want to graduate, I must take a course in auto mechanics. Part 5. 1. X; There are 2. C. 3. X; Is there 4. X; There are 5. X; How many pounds are there

Test 65 p. 115: Part 1. 1. Carol's last name is Barber. 2. Carol is — years old. (Answers will vary; subtract 1968 from the current year to find Carol's current age.) 3. Carol went to Hawaii on vacation. 4. Carol has two children. 5. Carol bought a dog in 1988. 6. Carol is going to visit Europe in 2010. 7. Carol has lived the longest in San Diego. Part 2. 1. C 2. B 3. D 4. B 5. B Part 3. 1. the, Leo's new car 2. The, yesterday's test 3. the players' good skills, the 4. the, Louisiana, Africa 5. the quality of this computer

Test 66 p. 117: Part 1. 1. B 2. B 3. A 4. B 5. A 6. A 7. B 8. B Part 2. 1. bigger 2. older 3. most intelligent 4. more 5. the happiest 6. more interesting

7. lighter 8. bigger Part 3. 1. —, a, —, —, —, a, a, the, the, — 2. —, the, the, the, —, the, the, the, —, the, —, the, —, — 3. the, the, An, the, the, —, a, the, an Part 4. 1. long, can 2. Almost, for 3. How come, wrote 4. usually eat, most 5. What, give, missing, another

Test 67 p. 119: 1. B 2. C 3. D 4. B 5. C 6. B 7. D 8. C 9. B 10. B 11. A 12. B 13. D 14. A 15. B 16. C 17. C 18. B 19. B 20. D

Test 68 p. 122: Part 1. 1. D 2. J 3. E 4. F 5. G 6. I 7. C 8. B 9. A 10. H Part 2. 1. up 2. on 3. on 4. on 5. out 6. up 7. up 8. off Part 3. 1. look my sister after = look after my sister 2. Put on it = Put it on 3. on = in 4. give away it = give it away 5. handed on = handed in 6. turn it the TV on = turn the TV on 7. calls his old high school friends on = calls on his old high school friends 8. ran her boss into = ran into her boss 9. looks it up = looks them up 10. get along him with = get along with him.

Test 69 p. 124: Part 1. 1. down 2. on 3. called 4. ran, up 5. on, put 6. off, turn 7. put 8. try 9. up, drop 10. up, away Part 2. 1. down 2. off 3. up 4. with 5. out 6. out 7. on 8. up 9. up 10. up 11. at 12. out

Test 70 p. 126: 1. A, B, D 2. A, C 3. A, B, C 4. C, D 5. B, C 6. B 7. B, C, D 8. A, B, C 9. B, C, D 10. C 11. A, C 12. B 13. A, B, C 14. A, B, C, D 15. A, C

Test 71 p. 129: Part 1. 1. C 2. B 3. D 4. A 5. A Part 2. 1. was listening 2. listened 3. played 4. was playing 5. baked 6. was baking 7. Were you driving 8. Did you drive 9. did not live 10. was not living

Test 72 p. 131: Part 1. 1. studied 2. was studying 3. were arguing, told 4. ate 5. were eating 6. was working 7. were traveling, ended 8. was practicing, began Part 2. 1. sang, were singing 2. drove, were driving 3. walked, was walking 4. read, was reading 5. listened, were listening 6. did, was doing 7. squeaked, was squeaking 8. cooked, were cooking 9. did not type, was not typing 10. lived, was living Part 3. 1. did not learn 2. was 3. was living 4. decided 5. failed 6. hit 7. passed 8. decided 9. was watching 10. chose 11. was going 12. drove

Test 73 p. 133: Part 1. 1. look out 2. run into 3. get through 4. put away 5. break up 6. put off 7. turn up 8. run out (of) 9. put back 10. look up Part 2. 1. away 2. across 3. on 4. in 5. out (OR in) 6. out 7. out Part 3. 1. was driving. 2. was washing, mopped. (OR was mopping.) 3. were taking, walked. (OR was walking.) 4. was playing. 5. was she thinking. Part 4. 1. Billy was studying for his exam from 12:00 P.M. to 2:30 P.M. 2. He was shopping for gifts from 3:00 to 5:30 P.M. 3. He was eating dinner from 6:00 to 6:30 P.M. 4. He was doing his homework from 7:00 to 9:00 P.M. 5. He was watching television from 9:00 to 11:00 P.M.

Test 74 p. 135: Part 1. 1. B 2. A 3. C 4. D 5. B Part 2. 1. was 2. traveled 3. landed 4. flew 5. is 6. made 7. went 8. was walking 9. ran into 10. are 11. was shooting 12. took 13. got 14. didn't regret

(OR don't regret) 15. look at Part 3. 1. Yesterday I went to the doctor. 2. What did you do last night at 7:00 P.M.? (OR What were you doing last night at 7:00 P.M.?) 3. She goes to work early and comes home late. 4. Joe washed the car, painted the house, and studied for exams last week. 5. While Mary was cleaning the house yesterday, her roommate watched (OR was watching) television.

Test 75 p. 137: Part 1. 1. called, was watching, called, tell, told, Do you want, am reading, am going to drive, 2. are going to go, have, do, 3. called, was, Did you go, went, was trying, wanted, go, saw, enjoys

Test 76 p. 139: Part 1. 1. C 2. B 3. C 4. D 5. A 6. A 7. C 8. B 9. A 10. C Part 2. 1. They were fighting when the police arrived. 2. We are going to go to the movies tonight. 3. They should apologize for being rude. 4. The goalie caught the soccer ball. 5. She talked to her mom last night.

Test 77 p. 141: Part 1. 1. begun 2. brought 3. bought 4. drunk 5. felt 6. known 7. seen 8. shown (OR showed, but only in perfect tenses) 9. spoken 10. written Part 2. 1. traveled 2. has traveled 3. have eaten 4. ate 5. has read 6. read 7. Did you sell 8. Have you sold 9. has, gone 10. went Part 3. 1. have you lived 2. has never seen 3. Did the boys come 4. has worn 5. got Part 4. 1. for 2. since 3. for 4. for 5. since

Test 78 p. 143: Part 1. 1. I haven't sung. Have I sung? 2. He hasn't driven. Has he driven? 3. We haven't chosen. Have we chosen? 4. They haven't fallen. Have they fallen? 5. You haven't eaten. Have you eaten? Part 2. 1. I have had a new house since 1997. 2. Juan has studied English for three years. 3. Nina has played the piano since 1972. 4. I have eaten sushi for (years will vary; subtract 1993 from the current year) years. 5. Nancy has worked at the university since (year will vary; subtract three from the current year). Part 3. 1. have met 2. came 3. has visited 4. went 5. had 6. took Part 4. 1. have worn 2. wore 3. caught 4. has caught 5. read 6. has read 7. have talked 8. talked

Test 79 p. 145: Part 1. 1. Bob speaks clearly. 2. They dance well. 3. He speaks Greek fluently. 4. She reads rapidly. 5. They take notes well. Part 2. 1. well 2. nervously 3. loud 4. hard 5. slowly 6. correctly 7. fast 8. quietly 9. badly 10. good Part 3. 1. by dieting 2. with a computer 3. By studying 4. by car 5. by not worrying about 6. with a reservation 7. By calling 8. with small tools 9. by boat 10. By not eating

Test 80 p. 147: Part 1. 1. beautifully 2. well 3. extremely 4. angrily 5. brightly 6. quickly 7. recently 8. stupidly 9. quietly 10. sadly 11. fast 12. newly 13. slowly 14. badly Part 2. 1. brightly 2. loud 3. good, easily 4. great, hard 5. recently 6. angrily 7. angry 8. silently, extremely 9. fast 10. bad Part 3. 1. by, by 2. with, with 3. with 4. by, by 5. by 6. with 7. by 8. with Part 4. 1. by cutting 2. by not studying 3. by using 4. by spending 5. to write 6. to see

Test 81 p. 149: Part 1. 1. Lucy hasn't woken up yet. 2. The boys haven't finished the test yet. 3. Rhonda

hasn't gone shopping yet. (OR Rhonda hasn't bought groceries yet.) 4. The twins haven't graduated from high school yet. 5. I haven't traveled to Morocco yet. (OR I haven't been in Morocco yet.) Part 2. 1. lives = lived (OR has lived, has been living) 2. ever see = have ever seen 3. ever drove = ever driven 4. didn't travel = haven't traveled 5. already saw = have already seen Part 3. 1. extremely 2. hard 3. By using 4. well 5. with our notes 6. terribly 7. easy 8. With your help 9. legibly 10. quickly

Test 82 p. 151: Part 1. 1. with 2. to, in, from 3. for, with 4. on, with 5. for, on Part 2. 1. C 2. B 3. D 4. B 5. D Part 3. 1. book full = book is full 2. is used to live = used to live 3. spill = spilling 4. to = about 5. for = to

Test 83 p. 153: Part 1. 1. to 2. for 3. on 4. to 5. of 6. about 7. of 8. on 9. for 10. about Part 2. 1. D 2. E 3. A 4. C 5. B Part 3. 1. to 2. to / with 3. by (OR at) 4. about 5. to 6. to 7. to (OR with) 8. about 9. for 10. about

Test 84 p. 155: Part 1. 1. I was born in 19__ __ . 2. I was born in Philadelphia (or another city or a country). 3. I was called _____ . Part 2. 1. was taken 2. is made, is cleaned, is done 3. finished 4. completed 5. was broken Part 3. 1. B 2. A 3. D 4. C 5. B Part 4. 1. in 1982 by a writer = in 1982 (omit the phrase "a writer" because this is not new information) 2. boring = bored 3. will married = will be (OR get) married 4. was happened = happened 5. was do = was done

Test 85 p. 157: Part 1. 1. were painted 2. was signed 3. was written 4. was being fixed 5. should be taken Part 2. 1. is hit 2. was injured 3. is teaching 4. must be made 5. must be followed 6. was arrested 7. are kept 8. is driving 9. have to practice 10. have I told Part 3. 1. is closed 2. are made 3. is divorced 4. are fried 5. is, cleaned 6. is gone 7. be bored 8. looked, received 9. was tired 10. was disappointed

Test 86 p. 159: Part 1. 1. at 2. with (OR in) 3. in 4. for 5. with 6. for 7. in 8. to 9. to 10. with Part 2. 1. A 2. D 3. B 4. C 5. B

Test 87 p. 161: Part 1. 1. The professor who (OR that) just started speaking is very famous. OR The professor who (OR that) is very famous just started talking. 2. The tiger which (OR that) escaped from the zoo was finally caught and killed. 3. This is a great park (OR which OR that) we used to visit all the time in college. 4. Police officers are honest people (whom OR who OR that) you can go to when you need help. 5. He turned in the homework which (OR that) was late this morning. Part 2. 1. X, you like (OR that you like OR who you like OR whom you like) 2. C 3. C 4. X, trip is 5. C 6. X, Whose Part 3. 1. Dali is a painter. 2. I don't know the person. 3. My friend's pet snake died last week. 4. I like to wear the blue bathing suit. 5. Who's the person?

Test 88 p. 162: Part 1. 1. who lives in the apartment above us 2. which stars Julia Roberts 3. that is found on that corner 4. whose grammar book we

use 5. that is on the bookshelf Part 2. 1. that 2. which 3. whose 4. that 5. which Part 3. 1. The architect designed a home which (OR that) is in the gothic style. 2. Here are the groceries I bought (OR that I bought OR which I bought). 3. The dog which (OR that) is wagging its tail is friendly. 4. People who (OR that) don't like snowstorms live in the south. 5. The music which (OR that) was played at the party last night was loud. Part 4. 1. that was 2. that are 3. who was 4. who are, who are 5. who were

Test 89 p. 164: 1. dating 2. dating 3. being 4. to follow 5. to be 6. to begin 7. losing 8. to do 9. smoking 10. to stop 11. quitting 12. confronting 13. dealing 14. smoking 15. Complaining 16. to see 17. Telling

Test 90 p. 166: Part 1. 1. to do 2. quitting, going 3. to play 4. talking 5. to listen Part 2. 1. to buy = buying 2. are = is 3. offered paying = offered to pay 4. to eat = eating 5. to do = doing Part 3. 1. I 2. B 3. I 4. G 5. I 6. B 7. B 8. G 9. I Part 4. 1. ✓ 2. — 3. — 4. ✓

Test 91 p. 167: Part 1. 1. to write 2. going 3. practicing 4. living 5. to pass 6. driving 7. transferring 8. skiing 9. to look for 10. eating Part 2. 1. B 2. F 3. E 4. D 5. C 6. A

Test 92 p. 168: Part 1. 1. who is standing on that corner 2. whose parents will not attend the play 3. that you wanted to buy 4. which is on the table 5. who do not do their homework Part 2. 1. The man who is holding the blue umbrella is my father. 2. The book that (OR which OR —) I am reading for English class is on the kitchen table. 3. The man who (OR that) was holding the winning lottery ticket looked very happy. 4. The dog that (OR which) was chasing the cat down the street is mine. 5. I played the violin that (OR which OR —) my uncle gave me. Part 3. 1. C 2. X; avoid drinking 3. X; put off mowing 4. C 5. X; refused to let Part 4. 1. to buy 2. Eating 3. to eat 4. to do 5. is 6. Tell 7. to take 8. to work

Test 93 p. 170: Part 1. 1. to (OR in order to) 2. to (OR in order to) 3. for 4. for 5. to (OR in order to) Part 2. 1. Espresso is very strong coffee, and so is Cuban coffee. (OR Espresso is very strong coffee, and Cuban coffee is too.) 2. Barbara doesn't have a cold, and neither does Warren. (OR Barbara doesn't have a cold, and Warren doesn't either.) 3. Brad has to write a report for class, and so do I. (OR Brad has to write a report for class, and I do too.) 4. They don't need to talk with the teacher, but Susan does. 5. I like to use the Internet to get information for my research papers, but I don't like to use the library. Part 3. 1. I studied very hard for my driver's license test; however, I failed it. 2. Bob opened the window so the air could come inside. 3. You need to pass the next test; therefore, you had better study very hard. 4. Jennifer wanted to take a

picture of her friend; however, her camera was broken.

Test 94 p. 172: Part 1. 1. to, to 2. for, to 3. for, to 4. to, for 5. to, for Part 2. 1. but 2. but 3. and 4. and 5. and Part 3. 1. and so does my sister, and my sister does too. 2. and neither are gorillas, and gorillas aren't either 3. and so is Arizona, and Arizona is also 4. and neither does Elias, and Elias doesn't either 5. and so did Nina, and Nina did too Part 4. 1. C 2. B 3. A

Test 95 p. 174: Part 1. 1. A 2. B 3. B 4. B 5. A Part 2. 1. opened the door to me = opened the door for me 2. introduce you Joe = introduce you to Joe 3. saves for me = saves me 4. written to me = written me 5. got for my mother = got my mother 6. passed the folder for Mr. Klein = passed the folder to Mr. Klein 7. explained me the algebra equation = explained the algebra equation to me 8. do for me a favor = do a favor for me (OR do me a favor) 9. find me them = find them for me 10. bought to his wife = bought his wife

Test 96 p. 176: Part 1. 1. B 2. B 3. A 4. B 5. A Part 2. 1. me 2. to me 3. for me 4. to me 5. me Part 3. 1. asked 2. gave 3. found 4. repeated 5. charged Part 4. 1. X; you your car? (OR your car to you?) 2. C 3. C 4. C 5. X; for me

Test 97 p. 178: Part 1. 1. to 2. for 3. to 4. to 5. for Part 2. 1. C 2. D 3. B 4. A 5. B Part 3. 1. to 2. for 3. — 4. to 5. for Part 4. 1. C 2. C 3. X; cost Ted 4. C 5. X; did my homework for me.

Test 98 p. 180: Part 1. 1. off 2. up 3. on 4. out 5. out Part 2. 1. flown, flew, was, was, made 2. is, have never seen, have you seen, was printing, is still Part 3. 1. with car = by car 2. engine careful = engine carefully 3. By do = By doing 4. efficient as = efficiently as 5. dangerously driving = dangerous driving Part 4. 1. of 2. to 3. for 4. about 5. about 6. of 7. of 8. to 9. of 10. from 11. with 12. of 13. at 14. of 15. to Part 5. 1. heard, was reported 2. were involved, stated 3. was broadcast 4. was hit 5. hit 6. was traveling, entered Part 6. 1. C 2. X; that he read 3. X; who live 4. C 5. C 6. X; areas which (OR that) have 7. C 8. C Part 7. 1. to do, to let, get, so, to me 2. but, me, strange, by, to do, either

Test 99 p. 183: 1. C, has had 2. enjoyed, by following 3. C, C 4. happened, C 5. accustomed to eating, but 6. were really bored, C 7. speaks slowly, easy to understand 8. C, woman whose husband 9. C, put them off for too long 10. To make, for 11. have been living (OR have lived), to keep on living 12. C, C 13. C, that Dr. Giles (OR which Dr. Giles OR Dr. Giles) 14. C, quickly left 15. annoying, heard

Test 100 p. 185: 1. C 2. D 3. B 4. D 5. A 6. A 7. D 8. B 9. D 10. B 11. C 12. A 13. A 14. B 15. A 16. D 17. C 18. D 19. C 20. D